HOW TO GROW SHRUBS AND CLIMBERS

A comprehensive guide to essential gardening techniques and skills,
from choosing, planting and growing to care and maintenance

Over 380 colour photographs with practical
and easy-to-follow advice

Jonathan Edwards

southwater

This edition is published by Southwater, an imprint of Anness Publishing Ltd, Hermes House, 88–89 Blackfriars Road, London SE1 8HA
tel. 020 7401 2077; fax 020 7633 9499

www.southwaterbooks.com; www.annesspublishing.com

If you like the images in this book and would like to investigate using them for publishing, promotions or advertising, please visit our website www.practicalpictures.com for more information.

UK agent: The Manning Partnership Ltd
tel. 01225 478444; fax 01225 478440; sales@manning-partnership.co.uk
UK distributor: Grantham Book Services Ltd
tel. 01476 541080; fax 01476 541061; orders@gbs.tbs-ltd.co.uk
North American agent/distributor: National Book Network
tel. 301 459 3366; fax 301 429 5746; www.nbnbooks.com
Australian agent/distributor: Pan Macmillan Australia
tel. 1300 135 113; fax 1300 135 103; customer.service@macmillan.com.au
New Zealand agent/distributor: David Bateman Ltd
tel. (09) 415 7664; fax (09) 415 8892

ETHICAL TRADING POLICY
At Anness Publishing we believe that business should be conducted in an ethical and ecologically sustainable way, with respect for the environment and a proper regard to the replacement of the natural resources we employ.
As a publisher, we use a lot of wood pulp to make high-quality paper for printing, and that wood commonly comes from spruce trees. We are therefore currently growing more than 500,000 trees in two Scottish forest plantations near Aberdeen – Berrymoss (130 hectares/320 acres) and West Touxhill (125 hectares/305 acres). The forests we manage contain twice the number of trees employed each year in paper-making for our books. Because of this ongoing ecological investment programme, you, as our customer, can have the pleasure and reassurance of knowing that a tree is being cultivated on your behalf to naturally replace the materials used to make the book you are holding.
Our forestry programme is run in accordance with the UK Woodland Assurance Scheme (UKWAS) and will be certified by the internationally recognized Forest Stewardship Council (FSC). The FSC is a non-government organization dedicated to promoting responsible management of the world's forests. Certification ensures forests are managed in an environmentally sustainable and socially responsible basis. For further information about this scheme, go to www.annesspublishing.com/trees

Previously published as part of a larger volume, *The Gardener's Guide to Shrubs & Climbers*

Publisher: Joanna Lorenz
Senior Managing Editor: Conor Kilgallon
Editors: Clare Hill and Elizabeth Woodland
Designer: Nigel Partridge
Cover Designer: Nigel Partridge
Production Controller: Don Campaniello

Contents

Introduction

Shrubs and climbers are the mainstay of the garden, providing structure and an ever-changing tapestry of colour throughout every month of the year. Their variety is both a delight and a dilemma – with so many to choose from there's almost certainly one to suit you and your garden, but the choice is so vast it can be totally bewildering.

Enjoying plants

Even if you stick to the basic fare offered by most garden centres, you may have 400 varieties of shrubs and nearly as many climbers to consider. So where do you start?

Well, not with an empty trolley at the garden centre, because impulse buys almost always lead to disappointing results. If you are planting a new border from scratch, buying all the plants in this way at best leads to a border that looks good at one time of year. The safest way to buy the right plant for your garden is to ask yourself the following questions while standing in your garden viewing your plot:

A garden only really comes together with maturity. This means that thought should be given to the eventual size and staying power of the plant when you are setting out your design.

Where is it to be planted?

Consider the amount of direct sun the plot gets; the type of soil and its condition; and the plot's exposure to wind, rain and cold. It is also worth noting the space available.

What will the plant's role in the garden be? Is it to fill a gap, add height and/or colour, extend the period of interest, cover the ground or a fence, hide an eyesore, act as a barrier or backdrop or is it to be used a specimen or focal point?

How quickly must it perform?

Do you want results in a year or two, or are you prepared to wait a little longer? Bear in mind that many fast-growing plants will continue to get bigger and so will either need regular pruning or moving. Others, such as *Lavatera*, are short-lived and will need replacing after a few years.

Any special requests?

In certain circumstances you might want to avoid certain plants. For example, if your gardening time is very limited or unpredictable, you might want to avoid high-maintenance plants that require a lot of pruning or training. On the other hand, if you have young children or young visitors, you should avoid or remove any poisonous plants that you have in your garden. With this

Climbers can be grown up exterior walls to hide eyesores such as outdoor pipes.

Clematis 'Comtesse de Bouchard' is ideal for growing against a sunny wall.

Rosa 'Queen of Denmark' is one of the finest old-fashioned shrub roses and is ideal for an open, sunny site. It is a vigorous, disease resistant plant.

Learning the ropes

There is no need to worry overly much about gardening techniques. Most gardening is common sense, and if you do make a mistake, you can always put it right the following year. Then again, there's a lot we can learn from the experience of past generations of gardeners, and their knowledge and expertise forms the basis of the advice given in this book.

Choosing and caring for plants

In the Choosing Shrubs and Climbers section you'll find plenty of suggestions for plants to suit your particular requirements, as well as useful lists of plants for each season of interest, colour and scent. Having chosen your plants you'll want to keep them healthy and performing well, and you'll find advice on planting, pruning and dealing with pests and diseases later in the book. There's also a section on propagation, so you can gain even more pleasure from your garden, as well as sharing plants with fellow enthusiasts.

information in mind, you are then in a position to draw up a shortlist of potential plant candidates. You can follow the same procedure when planning a whole border from scratch. The first three questions apply to the border as a whole, then the last can be considered for each individual element.

Working with colour

Many beginners are worried about combining colours, but the key is simply to go for plants and effects that you like, without worrying about what other people do.

Remember, we all have some ability where colour is concerned: we choose what goes with what when we get dressed every morning, and we choose colours for decorating and furnishing our home. Planning a garden is really no different. In the same way that there are fashion and style magazines to advise you about these areas of your life, there is no shortage of different types of gardening magazines to browse

through for inspiration – and there is nothing more enjoyable for the enthusiastic gardener than being able to wander around other people's gardens, horticultural displays or the grounds of stately homes in search of new ideas and planting styles.

Shrubs provide a multitude of different shapes, colours, textures and sizes. Blending them together, as shown by the variety of green backdrop foliage plants and trees above, allows the stunning hues of the *Daboecia cantabrica* 'Atropurpurea' pride of place in the foreground.

Choosing shrubs and climbers

To establish quickly, grow well and perform superbly, a new shrub or climber needs to be in the best possible condition when you buy it. However, even a top-quality plant will languish if it does not suit the conditions you have in your garden. For this reason, it is essential that you choose the right plant for the position you have in mind.

It is also worth considering how the plant will fit in with your existing garden residents. Some plants produce a spectacular but brief display, while others give a more restrained performance over a much longer period of time. A few plants are of particular value in the garden because they offer more than one season of interest, with summer flowers, autumn berries and foliage as well as colourful winter stems. It is also worth choosing reliable shrubs and climbers that are not susceptible to pest and disease.

If you are filling a new garden with shrubs and climbers, try to include a proportion of quick-growing plants, such as forsythia and buddleja, to give an instant display while the others are getting established.

The careful choosing, siting and nurturing of shrubs and climbers can produce the most stunning effects in the garden.

Buying shrubs and climbers

How well a new plant performs in your garden will depend largely on the quality and condition of the plant you buy. The following will provide a useful guide to choosing the best possible new candidate for your garden.

Check out the supplier

The most important advice to any would-be planter is to go to a reputable plant supplier. If they are known for offering good quality, well-looked-after and reasonably priced plants, the chances are you will not be disappointed.

However, even reputable garden centres, nurseries and internet suppliers can have their off days, particularly towards the end of a busy spring, when many essential tasks are put off, as well as towards the end of summer, when unsold stock has become pot-bound and running short of nutrients. The best time to visit a garden centre is early in the season, when they are up to date with their maintenance and stock. Ideally, find out which days they get their deliveries so that you will have the best choice possible.

One drawback with most garden centres is that they tend to have a very limited range of the most

Garden centres tend to stock the most popular and commonly available shrubs and climbers and will offer growing advice.

Choose the healthiest looking plants. Opt for those with a strong, bushy habit (centre) and avoid those with any signs of leaf yellowing (right). Plants with stunted, straggly growth (left) should be rejected, as should those with premature leaf fall.

popular and easy-to-propagate varieties, so if you want something a little unusual or are after a particular variety, you would be better off going to a specialist nursery.

If you are trying a new garden centre for the first time, walk around the plant beds and take an overall view. Look at plants you know, to check that the labels are correct and not faded – a tell-tale sign that the plant has been hanging around the outlet for too long.

Inspect the plant

Pots should be weed and moss free, and there should not be excessive roots coming out of the bottom of the pot – a tell-tale indication that the plant has been in the pot too long. On the other hand, a plant with loose compost is likely to have been potted only recently, which means it will need to be grown on in its pot until well established, before it is ready to plant out. If you are

unsure, ask if you can see the rootball to make certain the plant's roots have filled the pot but are not pot-bound.

Check the label before you buy, to see if the plant has any special soil requirements, then check to see if it needs to be planted in sun or shade. Also bear in mind that only fully hardy plants will survive outside all year round in cooler climates. If the information on the label is unclear or ambiguous, don't be afraid to ask for advice, or check out the information for yourself here, or in another reputable plant reference book.

Buying a climber

When bought during the growing season, the ideal climber should have several new stems that are putting on vigorous growth. New shoots should also be coming from near the base. Grafted climbers such as wisteria and budded climbers such as roses

Rootballed plants have a ball of soil around the roots and are protected by a covering of net or hessian.

Bare-rooted plants are usually sold covered with plastic wrapping. Keep the wrap intact until you are ready to plant.

foliage. If you are buying bare-rooted plants, the roots should be moist and well covered.

Getting your plants home

Once you have chosen your top-quality plants, don't destroy all your good work by damaging them on the way home. If you are transporting plants in cold weather, wrapping them in a blanket or bubble wrap not only provides good padding but also protects the plant from getting over-chilled. When buying in hot weather, avoid leaving plants in the car for any length of time, as the inside can turn into a furnace in sunny weather and may destroy the plants. Protect from direct sun by throwing a cover over them and make sure you drive them straight home, giving them a good drink of water when you arrive.

Small shrubs and climbers can be easily transported by car but tall plants need to be transported lying down. Cover them to stop the soil escaping and secure them to stop them from rolling around in the car.

should have a strong, well-healed union with all the stems coming from above it. Check that the shoots of all climbers are in good condition and not broken or damaged.

Another important point is that they should not be showing any signs of pest or disease attack. In particular, watch out for colonies of tiny insects in the growing tips (aphids) and white (mildew) or brown (leaf spots) patches on the leaves. On roses also look out for orange spots (rust) on the undersides of leaves.

Buying a shrub

A well-grown deciduous shrub should be roughly symmetrical, with vigorous, well-branched shoots. Evergreen shrubs should have healthy-looking foliage right down to the compost level.

Do not be seduced by buying big, as a small, vigorous shrub will establish itself more quickly than a larger shrub, and it will soon catch up in size when it is planted in the border. By buying small, you'll save money, too. The only exceptions to this rule are for very slow-growing

shrubs, such as acers, which are worth buying larger, and flowering shrubs that you want for providing an instant display in a prominent container on the patio.

As with climbers, you should check for any signs of pests or disease and watch out for all-green shoots on variegated varieties. Avoid shrubs with withered or yellow

Specialist nurseries carry a wider range of shrubs and climbers. Plants can also be ordered from catalogues or bought via the Internet. This is especially helpful if you are after a plant that is unusual or not carried by your local garden centre.

Plant selector: multi-season interest

The following Plant Selector has been structured to make choosing the right plants for your garden as easy as possible. There are Selectors for each season and colour, as well as for scent. However, we must first look at those plants that offer particular garden value, because they provide a range of different ornamental features that enable them to spread their period of interst over two or more seasons.

Location, location

Shrubs and climbers are permanent additions to your garden, so it is important that you not only choose the right plant for a particular spot but also select a good variety that can justify itself. Over the next few pages some of the best garden shrubs and climbers for every season have been outlined, but first we must consider the few highly rated shrubs and climbers that offer two, three or even four seasons of interest.

The impressive coral-bark maple, *Acer palmatum* 'Sango-kaku', provides year-round interest in this way and is an ideal choice for small gardens. The brilliant coral-red young shoots dramatically set off the emerging palm-shaped, orange-yellow leaves in spring. Then the leaves gradually turn green in summer, before taking

Viburnum opulus 'Roseum' produces big, white, snowball-like blooms in late spring.

Multi-season shrubs and climbers to try

Shrubs

Acer palmatum 'Osakazuki' (leaves, fruits, autumn colour)
Acer palmatum 'Sango-kaku' (leaves, stems, new shoots, autumn colour)
Amelanchier lamarckii (leaves, flowers, autumn colour)
Berberis darwinii (leaves, flowers, berries)
Cornus alba cultivars (leaves, stems, flowers, autumn colour)
Cornus sanguinea 'Midwinter Fire' (leaves, stems, flowers, fruits, autumn colour)
Corylus maxima 'Purpurea' (leaves, flowers, nuts)
Cotinus coggygria 'Royal Purple' (leaves, flowers, autumn colour)
Cotoneaster horizontalis (leaves, flowers, fruit)
Daphne mezereum (leaves, flowers, berries)
Fatsia japonica (leaves, flowers)
Hamamelis mollis 'Pallida' (flowers, leaves, autumn colour)
Hydrangea quercifolia (leaves, flowers, autumn colour)
Mahonia japonica (leaves, flowers, fruits)
Rhamnus alaternus 'Argenteovariegata' (leaves, flowers)
Rhododendron luteum (leaves, flowers, autumn colour)
Rhus typhina 'Dissecta' (leaves, stems, new shoots, autumn colour)
Rosa 'Blanche Double de Coubert' (leaves, flowers, hips, autumn colour)
Rosa rugosa 'Rubra' (leaves, flowers, hips, autumn colour)

Skimmia japonica 'Rubella' (leaves, flower-buds, flowers)
Viburnum opulus 'Roseum' (leaves, flowers, fruit, autumn colour)
Viburnum plicatum 'Mariesii' (leaves, flowers, fruit, autumn colour)

Climbers

Akebia quinata (flowers, foliage)
Aristolochia macrophylla (flowers, foliage, autumn colour)
Clematis alpina cultivars (leaves, flowers, seed-heads)
Clematis 'Bill MacKenzie' (leaves, flowers, seedheads)
Clematis tangutica (leaves, flowers, seed-heads)
Hedera helix 'Green Ripple' (leaves, winter colour)
Hydrangea petiolaris (leaves, flowers, seed-heads, autumn colour)
Parthenocissus henryana (leaves, autumn colour)
Passiflora caerulea (leaves, flowers, fruit)
Rosa filipes 'Kiftsgate' (flowers, hips)
Rosa 'Madame Grégoire Staechelin' (flowers, hips)
Rosa 'Rambling Rector' (flowers, hips)
Sollya heterophylla (flowers, foliage, fruit)
Vitis coignetiae (leaves, autumn colour, fruit)
Vitis vinifera 'Purpurea' (leaves, autumn colour, fruit)
Wisteria floribunda (leaves, flowers, pods, autumn colour)

---

on fabulous shades of yellow in autumn, falling to reveal the coloured stems through winter.

Another deciduous shrub that provides year-round interest is the dogwood *Cornus sanguinea* 'Midwinter Fire'. This relatively new cultivar bears clusters of tiny, creamy-white flowers during early summer, against green leaves that transform in autumn, when they take on orange-yellow hues and when spherical

bluish fruits are also produced. But it is in winter that it really comes to the fore, revealing spectacular glowing, red-tipped, orange and yellow winter stems that shine out in the winter garden.

In a larger garden, the snowy mespilus, *Amelanchier lamarckii*, provides excellent value. It is a spectacular shrub at both ends of the growing season and is covered in a profusion of star-shaped, white flowers accompanied by bronze-tinted emerging leaves during spring. In autumn, the dark-green foliage transforms into a beacon of orange and red. Sweet and juicy dark red fruits are also produced during early summer.

The purple-leaved smoke bush, *Cotinus coggygria* 'Royal Purple', makes an impressive specimen in any size of garden as it responds particularly well to hard pruning each spring. Airy plumes of pale pink flowers that darken with age are produced from mid-summer. The rich, red-purple leaves offer a colourful point of focus in the summer shrubbery or mixed garden border before turning brilliant scarlet in autumn.

Although the stag's horn sumach, *Rhus typhina*, has developed a troublesome reputation for suckering, the named cultivar 'Dissecta' is less of a problem and has the bonus of more finely cut, decorative foliage. Like the species, it also offers velvet-covered, red winter shoots as well as foliage that turns fiery shades of orange-red in the autumn. Spectacular bristly fruits

The Japanese *Acer palmatum* 'Osakazuki' will brighten up any garden, particularly during the autumn when its leaves turn a rich, vibrant red.

follow insignificant mustard flowers on conical spikes during the summer. The ornamental buckthorn *Rhamnus alaternus* 'Argenteovariegata' is worth a mention for its year-round white-edged evergreen foliage and red fruits that ripen to black in autumn.

The oak-leaved hydrangea, *Hydrangea quercifolia*, is a good garden shrub, offering attractive oak-leaf-shaped foliage that turns shades of bronze-purple in autumn. But it is the named cultivar 'Snow Queen' that steals the show, with its brilliant white conical flower clusters, produced in summer, that fade to pink as they age.

Another deciduous favourite that provides good colour is the Japanese snowball bush *Viburnum plicatum* 'Mariesii'. This produces tiered branches that carry white, lacecap-like flowers throughout late spring over toothed, prominently veined, dark-green leaves that turn red-purple in autumn.

A few climbers also offer year-round interest. Evergreens, such as ivy, are more or less ubiquitous, but for real garden value you want ever-changing displays like that offered by the climbing hydrangea, *Hydrangea petiolaris*, which bears huge, flat heads of creamy, lacecap flowers that stand out against a backdrop of dark green leaves from late spring. Then in autumn, the leaves turn butter-yellow before falling to reveal attractively flaking brown bark.

Clematis 'Bill MacKenzie' and *C. tangutica* are worth mentioning in this respect, too. The former produces butter-yellow, bell-shaped flowers in succession from mid-summer against ferny, mid-green leaves, followed by large, fluffy seed-heads, while the latter offers small, nodding, yellow, lantern-shaped flowers with waxy-looking lemon peel-like petals from mid-summer, again followed by fluffy seed-heads later on.

The autumn leaf colours of *Cotinus obovatus* can be yellow, red, orange or reddish-purple.

Plant selector: late spring

In some years, spring can be delayed for several weeks so keep an eye on local weather forecasts and gauge the temperature. Use these as a guide to your gardening activities, rather than doing things just because it is the season to do them.

Protect your plants

By late spring, the threat of frost recedes and in milder areas it's safe to plant out tender shrubs and climbers, but always keep a sheet of garden fleece to hand to cover vulnerable plants if an unseasonally late frost is forecast after planting has taken place.

Variations in weather conditions are generally less marked as the spring progresses, so there are fewer sharp frosts and the weather generally becomes calmer. In cooler areas, however, you will have to be a good deal more cautious and should wait until early summer to put tender plants outside.

Growth spurts

In the garden, shrubs and climbers are making up for lost time as they break into growth and compete for your attention.

Camellia x *williamsii* 'Jury's Yellow' has creamy-yellow, anemone-shaped blooms.

Late spring shrubs and climbers to try

Shrubs

Berberis darwinii
Berberis linearifolia 'Orange King'
Berberis thunbergii 'Atropurpurea Nana'
Berberis thunbergii 'Aurea'
Berberis x *stenophylla*
Berberis x *stenophylla* 'Crawley Gem'
Berberis x *stenophylla* 'Irwinii'
Calluna vulgaris 'Spring Cream'
Camellia japonica 'Adolphe Audusson'
Camellia japonica 'Elegans'
Camellia japonica 'Lady Vansittart'
Camellia 'Leonard Messel'
Camellia x *williamsii* 'Debbie'
Camellia x *williamsii* 'Donation'
Camellia x *williamsii* 'E.G. Waterhouse'
Camellia x *williamsii* 'J. C. Williams'
Camellia x *williamsii* 'Jury's Yellow'
Ceanothus 'Puget Blue'
Chaenomeles speciosa 'Geisha Girl'
Chaenomeles speciosa 'Moerloosei'
Chaenomeles speciosa 'Nivalis'
Chaenomeles x *superba* 'Crimson and Gold'
Chaenomeles x *superba* 'Nicoline'
Chaenomeles x *superba* 'Pink Lady'
Choisya 'Aztec Pearl'
Choisya 'Goldfingers'
Choisya ternata
Choisya ternata 'Sundance'
Cytisus multiflorus
Cytisus x *praecox* 'Allgold'
Cytisus x *praecox* 'Warminster'
Drimys winteri
Exochorda x *macrantha* 'The Bride'
Forsythia x *intermedia* 'Lynwood'
Fothergilla major
Leucothoe fontanesiana 'Rainbow'
Magnolia 'Heaven Scent'
Magnolia stellata 'Royal Star'
Magnolia x *loebneri* 'Leonard Messel'
Magnolia x *soulangeana*
Osmanthus delavayi
Osmanthus x *burkwoodii*
Paeonia delavayi
Paeonia lutea var. *ludlowii*
Paeonia suffruticosa 'Duchess of Kent'
Paeonia suffruticosa 'Duchess of Marlborough'
Paeonia suffruticosa 'Mrs William Kelway'
Paeonia suffruticosa 'Reine Elisabeth'
Pieris formosa var. *forrestii* 'Wakehurst'

Pieris 'Forest Flame'
Pieris japonica 'Purity'
Pieris japonica 'Variegata'
Prunus laurocerasus 'Otto Luyken'
Prunus laurocerasus 'Rotundifolia'
Prunus laurocerasus 'Zabeliana'
Prunus lusitanica
Rhododendron 'Blue Diamond'
Rhododendron 'Glowing Embers'
Rhododendron 'Grumpy'
Rhododendron 'Koster's Brilliant Red'
Rhododendron 'Persil'
Rhododendron 'Pink Drift'
Rhododendron 'Pink Pearl'
Rhododendron 'Sapphire'
Rhododendron 'Scarlet Wonder'
Ribes sanguineum 'Brocklebankii'
Ribes sanguineum 'King Edward VII'
Ribes sanguineum 'Pulborough Scarlet'
Salix lanata
Skimmia japonica subsp. *reevesiana*
Skimmia japonica subsp. *reevesiana* 'Robert Fortune'
Sophora microphylla
Sophora microphylla 'Sun King'
Spiraea 'Arguta'
Spiraea thunbergii
Viburnum carlesii
Viburnum 'Eskimo'
Viburnum x *burkwoodii*
Viburnum x *carlcephalum*
Viburnum x *juddii*
Vinca major
Vinca minor 'Illumination'

Climbers

Clematis alpina 'Frances Rivis'
Clematis alpina 'Frankie'
Clematis alpina 'Pamela Jackman'
Clematis alpina 'Pink Flamingo'
Clematis 'Early Sensation'
Clematis 'Helsingborg'
Clematis macropetala 'Markham's Pink'
Jasminum polyanthum
Lonicera japonica 'Halliana'
Lonicera japonica 'Hall's Prolific'
Lonicera japonica var. *repens*

Rhododendron 'Pink Pearl' is a delightful plant, bearing huge trusses of beautiful soft pink, funnel-shaped flowers that eventually fade to white as they age.

Many of the early flowering shrubs, including camellias and magnolias, are still going strong, but they are joined by equally impressive displays from popular plants such as peonies and rhododendrons. Perhaps the best peony of all is 'Ludlowii', which looks magnificent when furnished with large bright yellow flowers against bronze-tinted, bright apple-green lush foliage. If you are looking for a red, consider *Paeonia delavayi* instead, for its single, cup-shaped, blood-red flowers. Pale pink peonies are always popular, and the flamboyant 'Duchess of Marlborough', with its double, crinkle-edged flowers, is hard to beat.

Dramatic plants

There's a huge array of dramatic rhododendrons to choose from that will to add flower power to a late spring garden. Evergreen rhododendrons include the unusual violet-blue shade of 'Blue Diamond', which bears masses of funnel-shaped, flowers that age to lavender-blue. 'Grumpy' offers attractive pink-flushed, cream flowers in flat-topped trusses, while the compact 'Pink Drift' blooms are a rose-lavender shade – a good choice for small gardens. Well liked for good reason are the white-edged, soft pink, funnel-shaped flowers of 'Pink Pearl'.

Vivid azaleas

Deciduous azaleas come into bloom during late spring, too. The aptly named 'Glowing Embers' shows off its flaming, reddish-orange, funnel-shaped flowers, while 'Koster's Brilliant Red' offers vivid, orange-red blooms. For large clusters of orange-flushed, white flowers, look no further than the brilliant 'Persil'.

The appeal of flowering quince can be an acquired taste, but they'll never let you down with their startling flowers on a twiggy framework, often followed by aromatic, yellow-tinged green fruit. Good names to look out for at this time of the year are the apricot-pink and yellow, double flowers of 'Geisha Girl', the large white, apple blossom-like blooms of 'Moerloosei', the snow-white 'Nivalis' or the scarlet 'Nicoline'. But, perhaps the pick of the bunch is the compact and easy to grow 'Crimson and Gold'. This offers vivid red flowers with contrasting golden anthers.

Another late spring stalwart if you have an acid soil is the lily-of-the-valley shrub, pieris. It's particularly remarkable because it bears its pendent clusters of fragrant, urn-shaped flowers just when the glossy, brilliant-red young foliage emerges – a startling contrast that works perfectly together. 'Wakehurst', 'Forest Flame' and 'Purity' are all good white cultivars, while 'Valley Valentine' is dark pink.

Spring climbers

Popular climbers that are on display in the late spring garden include the many forms of alpine clematis, which bear small, nodding, bell-shaped flowers, often with contrasting centres. Look out for 'Frances Rivis' (blue), 'Helsingborg' (deep purple) and 'Pink Flamingo' (pink). Other floriferous early clematis that are at their best right now are: 'Early Sensation', which bears a single flush of small, green-centred, white, bowl-shaped flowers, and the semi-double 'Markham's Pink', which offers pink flowers with creamy-yellow centres.

Pieris 'Forest Flame' has glorious red leaves that fade to a pale pink and then dark green.

fragrant, double, rose-pink flowers; and 'Sussex', the slightly fragrant, double, apricot version.

Beneficial insects

Many other late-summer flowering shrubs provide a rich source of food for beneficial insects. Perhaps the most well known is the butterfly bush, *Buddleja davidii*, which bears dense terminal spikes of fragrant flowers that are a magnet to butterflies: 'Black Knight' (dark purple), 'Nanho Blue' (lilac-blue), 'Pink Delight' (orange-eyed, bright-pink flowers), 'White Profusion' (white) and the variegated 'Harlequin' (reddish-purple).

English lavenders are also covered in insects at this time of the year when they bear their very fragrant flowers in dense spikes. Cultivars to look out for include: 'Hidcote' (dark violet), 'Hidcote Pink' (pale pink), 'Lady' (mauve-blue) 'Nana Alba' (white) and 'Royal Purple' (bluish-purple).

Unusual shrubs

Slightly more unusual shrubs that are looking their best right now include the hare's ear, *Bupleurum*

Hydrangea macrophylla

fruticosum, which bears greenish-yellow, ball-shaped clusters of star-shaped flowers on a dense and spreading evergreen shrub with dark green leaves that are silvery on the

underside. Another excellent choice is the bladder plant, *Colutea arborescens*, which has racemes of bright yellow flowers followed by green seed-pods that become bloated and translucent as they mature. Highly recommended is hibiscus, particularly the delightful 'Blue Bird', which bears violet-blue, trumpet-shaped flowers, each with a maroon eye, in succession throughout late summer.

Finally, consider the white, tissue paper-like flowers, each with a golden-yellow centre, of *Romneya coulteri* 'White Cloud'.

Flowering structures

Walls and fences can be covered in flowers at this time of year, many of them sweetly fragrant. You can choose from a huge range of late-

Oleria x haastii

Rosa 'Golden Showers'

Rosa 'Gloire de Dijon'

flowering, large-flowered clematis, climbing and rambler roses and sweetly fragrant honeysuckles, such as: 'Graham Thomas', with large, tubular white flowers that age to yellow; 'Dropmore Scarlet,' which bears a succession of long, trumpet-shaped, bright-scarlet flowers; and 'Serotina', the late Dutch honeysuckle, which bears tubular, purple-streaked, creamy-white blooms.

Late summer climbers to try

Campsis grandiflora
Campsis radicans 'Flamenco'
Campsis x *tagliabuana* 'Madame Galen'
Clematis 'Alba Luxurians'
Clematis 'Betty Corning'
Clematis 'Bill MacKenzie'
Clematis 'Comtesse de Bouchaud'
Clematis 'Ernest Markham'
Clematis 'Etoile Violette'
Clematis flammula
Clematis 'Gipsy Queen'
Clematis 'Hagley Hybrid'
Clematis 'Henryi'
Clematis 'Huldine'
Clematis 'Jackmanii'
Clematis 'Jackmanii Superba'
Clematis 'Niobe'
Clematis 'Perle d'Azur'
Clematis 'Polish Spirit'
Clematis 'Prince Charles'
Clematis 'Princess Diana'
Clematis 'Rouge Cardinal'
Clematis tangutica
Clematis 'Ville de Lyon'
Clematis viticella 'Purpurea Plena Elegans'
Fallopia baldschuanica
Jasminum officinale 'Devon Cream'
Lapageria rosea
Lonicera periclymenum 'Graham Thomas'
Lonicera periclymenum 'Serotina'
Lonicera x *brownii* 'Dropmore Scarlet'

Mandevilla boliviensis
Mandevilla splendens
Mandevilla x *amabilis* 'Alice du Pont'
Passiflora caerulea
Passiflora caerulea 'Constance Elliot'
Passiflora 'Eden'
Pileostegia viburnoides
Rosa 'Aloha'
Rosa 'Bantry Bay'
Rosa 'Breath of Life'
Rosa 'Climbing Iceberg'
Rosa 'Compassion'
Rosa 'Danse du Feu'
Rosa filipes 'Kiftsgate'
Rosa 'Gloire de Dijon'
Rosa 'Golden Showers'
Rosa 'Handel'
Rosa 'Laura Ford'
Rosa 'Madame Alfred Carrière'
Rosa 'Mermaid'
Rosa 'New Dawn'
Rosa 'Rambling Rector'
Rosa 'Schoolgirl'
Rosa 'Warm Welcome'
Rosa 'Wedding Day'
Schizophragma hydrangeoides
Schizophragma integrifolium
Trachelospermum asiaticum
Trachelospermum jasminoides

Clematis viticella 'Purpurea Plena Elegans'

Trachelospermum asiaticum

Passiflora caerulea

Plant selector: autumn

Although warm weather can continue into early autumn in some years, this time of the year usually sees a dramatic change in both the weather and the appearance of the garden.

Shorter days and cool, longer nights are certain, causing plants to slow down and gradually become dormant. The autumn garden is briefly dominated by the fiery displays of many deciduous shrubs and climbers.

The acers

Some of the most spectacular autumn hues are offered by Japanese maples. Cultivars such as *Acer palmatum* 'Atropurpureum' make a graceful and slow-growing maple, with attractive palm-like, deeply lobed, dark purple leaves that are eye-catching all summer before turning brilliant shades of red in autumn. Another purple-leaved cultivar worth seeking out is 'Bloodgood', which turns brilliant red before falling. The startling red autumn colour of 'Osakazuki' is equally spectacular and would make a dramatic addition to any garden. If you prefer one of the cut-leaved varieties of Japanese

Abutilon megapotanicum 'Variegata'

maples, look out for *Acer palmatum* var. *dissectum* Dissectum Atropurpureum Group, which makes a neat dome covered in particularly fine, deeply cut, red-purple, ferny foliage that turns fiery shades in autumn. 'Garnet' is similar, but the foliage is darker purple. Both these cultivars look good after leaf fall, too, as they reveal a tracery of fine twigs that provide winter interest.

Others that offer excellent autumn shades are the barberry (*Berberis*) cultivars, such as 'Atropurpurea Nana', which is grown for its dark purple leaves that turn a brilliant red in autumn accompanied by glossy red fruits; by contrast 'Aurea' offers brilliant acid-yellow spring growth that turns orange-red in autumn with conspicuous glossy red fruit; 'Bagatelle' is compact and easy to grow, with dark purple leaves that transform into a stunning red in autumn; 'Dart's Red Lady' is equally suitable for a confined space and has plum-red foliage that turns brilliant shades of red at this time of the year. If you're looking for a columnar version, try 'Helmond Pillar', which is clothed in plum-purple leaves that take truly eye-catching shades of red in autumn.

Brilliant autumn foliage is also the main ornamental feature of *Cotinus*, the smoke bush. Excellent purple-leaved versions include 'Grace' and 'Royal Purple', which spectacularly turn fiery shades of red and orange during the autumn.

Enkianthus perulatus

Cotinus coggygria 'Golden Spirit' is a relatively new and compact cultivar with golden-yellow leaves that take on eye-catching pink, orange and red coloration at this time of the year. The hardy plumbago, *Ceratostigma willmottianum*, is also worth considering because it makes a neat mound covered in clusters of pale blue summer flowers and brilliant fiery foliage effects in autumn. Look out for 'Forest Blue', which turns flaming shades of red and orange at the end of the growing season.

Fruits of autumn

Autumn is also a time for bountiful fruit production and few plants can match the startling displays offered by the beauty bush, *Callicarpa bodinieri* var. *giraldii* 'Profusion', which bears astonishingly vibrant violet, bead-like berries. *Hippophae rhamnoides* is equally dramatic, forming a large, bushy plant with sharp spines and silvery lance-shaped leaves that fall in autumn to reveal the clusters of bright orange berries, that last well into winter. Don't overlook firethorn (*Pyracantha*) and cotoneasters as they produce long-lasting, glossy, brightly coloured berries. *C.* 'Coral Beauty' makes excellent ground cover for sun or semi-shade and is covered in glossy, bright-orange berries during the autumn.

The popular herringbone cotoneaster, *Cotoneaster horizontalis*, is encrusted with spherical, bright-red berries during the autumn. *C.* 'Cornubia' is an upright, evergreen cultivar that is often trained as a single-stemmed tree and is covered in spherical, bright-red berries just as the leaves become bronze-tinted for the winter; while 'Hybridus Pendulus' is lower growing and produces glossy, bright red berries at this time of the year.

Autumn shrubs and climbers to try

Shrubs
Acer palmatum 'Atropurpureum'
Acer palmatum 'Bloodgood'
Acer palmatum 'Orange Dream'
Acer palmatum 'Osakazuki'
Acer palmatum var. *dissectum* Dissectum Atropurpureum Group
Acer palmatum 'Garnet'
Amelanchier lamarckii
Amelanchier x grandiflora 'Ballerina'
Aucuba japonica 'Rozannie'
Aucuba japonica 'Variegata'
Berberis julianae
Berberis thunbergii 'Atropurpurea Nana'
Berberis thunbergii 'Aurea'
Berberis thunbergii 'Bagatelle'
Berberis thunbergii 'Dart's Red Lady'
Berberis thunbergii 'Helmond Pillar'
Berberis thunbergii f. *atropurpurea*
Callicarpa bodinieri var. *giraldii* 'Profusion'
Callistemon rigidus
Calluna vulgaris 'Alicia'
Calluna vulgaris 'Amethyst'
Calluna vulgaris 'County Wicklow'
Calluna vulgaris 'Dark Star'
Calluna vulgaris 'H. E. Beale'
Calluna vulgaris 'Silver Knight'
Calluna vulgaris 'Spring Cream'
Camellia sasanqua 'Narumigata'
Caryopteris x clandonensis
Caryopteris x clandonensis 'First Choice'
Caryopteris x clandonensis 'Heavenly Blue'

Caryopteris x clandonensis 'Worcester Gold'
Ceanothus 'Autumnal Blue'
Ceratostigma griffithii
Ceratostigma willmottianum
Ceratostigma willmottianum 'Desert Skies'
Ceratostigma willmottianum 'Forest Blue'
Clerodendrum trichotomum var. *fargesii*
Colutea arborescens
Colutea x media 'Copper Beauty'
Cornus alba 'Spaethii'
Cornus 'Eddie's White Wonder'
Cornus sanguinea 'Midwinter Fire'
Cotinus coggygria 'Golden Spirit'
Cotinus coggygria' Royal Purple'
Cotinus 'Flame'
Cotinus 'Grace'
Enkianthus perulatus
Fothergilla gardenii
Gaultheria mucronata 'Mulberry Wine'
Gaultheria mucronata 'Wintertime'
Gaultheria procumbens
Hippophae rhamnoides
Viburnum x bodnantense 'Dawn'
Viburnum x bodnantense 'Charles Lamont'

Climbers
Parthenocissus henryana
Parthenocissus quinquefolia
Vitis 'Brant'
Vitis coignetiae

Foliage climbers

Some climbers also offer glorious autumnal foliage displays. For example, the ornamental grape vine, *Vitis* 'Brant', has apple-green leaves that turn rust-red between the main veins in autumn, while the crimson glory vine, *Vitis coignetiae*, is absolutely spectacular when its dark green leaves turn fiery shades of red during the autumn.

On the other hand, Chinese Virginia creeper, *Parthenocissus henryana*, offers handsome, deeply divided, dark green leaves with distinctive white and pink veins that turn fiery shades before falling at the end of the growing season. The related Virginia creeper (*P. quinquefolia*) is clothed in deeply divided, slightly puckered green leaves that transform themselves during the autumn when they take on brilliant shades of crimson and purple.

Other varieties of creeper to look out for include *Parthenocissus* 'Robusta' and *P.* 'Veitchii', both of which transform themselves at this time of the year and develop a spectacular cloak of red and purple.

Colour selector: yellow

Warm and inviting, yellow is many a gardener's favourite flower colour. It seems to shine out in all weathers and at all times of the year.

Welcome yellow

In the spring, autumn and winter, yellow is a welcome relief on dreary days, radiating its cheerful disposition to all its neighbours. Then, in summer, it can be used to light up borders in both sun and dappled shade – contrasting the dark shadows where the sun is at its most fierce and reflecting light all around where it is not.

All yellows are fairly easy to accommodate into border schemes, combining well with oranges and reds to create hot, fiery displays, as well as providing startling contrasts to purples, violets and black. Yellow also partners browns and bronze shades to good effect, while white is a natural bedfellow.

Any yellow will happily partner green, which lies adjacent to it on the colour wheel, and some shades of yellow can be successfully added to schemes predominantly based on blue and silver tones. Even a monochrome display using a variety

Hypericum 'Hidcote'

of yellow hues can work particularly well. Choose two or three distinct, but complementary shades, such as the palest lemon-yellow, a clear butter-yellow and a rich bronzy-yellow. Being so accommodating, yellow is easy to take for granted. If it is used too liberally it dominates the whole garden display. However, there are so many shades of yellow that allow you to create subtly different effects around the garden without the effect being monotonous.

Yellow variegated foliage

Another way to introduce yellow into your garden is by using shrubs and climbers with yellow-variegated foliage. The effect you achieve will depend on the plants you choose and the plants that surround them. Yellow-variegated foliage ranges from the subtle greenish shades to the dramatic eye-catching tones of some all-yellow foliage plants. It is tempting to include yellow-variegated plants in monochrome schemes of yellow flowers, but this seldom works in practice because displays lack contrast and the various elements tend to cancel each other out. However, you can add a few pale yellow flowers to an all-yellow foliage scheme to good effect if you are aiming for a soothing, low-key combination.

Warm yellow

There is a huge range of plants that produce yellow flowers or foliage. You can start the year with the densely packed, arching spikes of the fragrant butter-yellow flowers of *Mahonia aquifolium* 'Apollo', which appear above the holly-like leaves that have a reddish tinge in winter. The stunning flower power of forsythias light up the spring with

Berberis 'Goldilocks'

their brilliant blooms produced *en masse* on bare stems. Among the best varieties are 'Beatrix Farrand' (orange-yellow), 'Lynwood' (golden-yellow), 'Spring Glory' (pale yellow), and 'Week End' (rich yellow). The deciduous azalea, *Rhododendron luteum*, is worth seeking out for its spectacular early summer, sweetly scented, yellow, funnel-shaped blooms. Another sought-after yellow is produced by *Fremontodendron* 'California Glory', which bears eye-catching, saucer-shaped, butter-yellow, waxy-looking flowers from late spring to autumn against a backdrop of leathery, lobed, dark green leaves.

Butter yellow

A spectacular seasonal highlight is produced by *Genista lydia*, when its arching stems are festooned in golden-yellow flowers throughout early summer. For larger, bright-yellow flowers at this time of year, you could opt for *Potentilla fruticosa* 'Goldfinger', which bears a crop of blooms against a mound of small, dark green leaves. You could also try *Hypericum* 'Hidcote', which bears impressive cup-shaped, golden-yellow flowers in succession from mid-

Yellow shrubs and climbers to try

Shrubs

Abelia x *grandiflora* 'Francis Mason'
Abelia x grandiflora 'Gold Spot'
Abutilon megapotamicum 'Variegatum'
Acer palmatum 'Sango-kaku'
Acer palmatum var. *dissectum* 'Ornatum'
Aucuba japonica 'Crotonifolia'
Aucuba japonica 'Picturata'
Azara dentata
Berberis aristata
Berberis thunbergii 'Aurea'
Berberis thunbergii 'Helmond Pillar'
Berberis x *stenophylla*
Berberis x *stenophylla* 'Claret Cascade'
Berberis x *stenophylla* 'Corallina
    Compacta'
Brachyglottis compacta 'Sunshine'
Buddleja davidii 'Harlequin'
Bupleurum fruticosum
Calluna vulgaris 'Wickwar Flame'
Caryopteris x *clandonensis* 'Worcester
    Gold'
Chimonanthus praecox
Chimonanthus praecox 'Grandiflorus'
Chimonanthus praecox 'Luteus'
Choisya 'Goldfingers'
Choisya ternata 'Sundance'
Colutea arborescens
Cornus alba 'Aurea'
Cornus stolonifera 'Flaviramea'
Coronilla valentina subsp. *glauca*
Cotinus coggygria 'Golden Spirit'
Cytisus battandieri
Cytisus x *praecox* 'Allgold'
Cytisus x *praecox* 'Warminster'
Diervilla x *splendens*
Elaeagnus pungens 'Maculata'
Elaeagnus x *ebbingei* 'Gilt Edge'
Elaeagnus x *ebbingei* 'Limelight'
Enkianthus campanulatus
Euonymus fortunei 'Emerald 'n' Gold'
Euonymus fortunei 'Sunspot'
Forsythia 'Beatrix Farrand'
Forsythia x *intermedia* 'Spring Glory'
Forsythia x *intermedia* 'Week End'
Fremontodendron 'California Glory'

Berberis aristata

Genista lydia
Genista pilosa 'Vancouver Gold'
Genista tinctoria 'Royal Gold'
Hamamelis x *intermedia* 'Moonlight'
Hamamelis x *intermedia* 'Pallida'
Hebe ochracea 'James Stirling'
Helianthemum 'Wisley Primrose'
Hypericum calycinum
Hypericum 'Hidcote'
Hypericum x *moserianum* 'Tricolor'
Ilex aquifolium 'Golden Queen'
Ilex x *altaclerensis* 'Golden King'
Jasminum nudiflorum
Kerria japonica 'Golden Guinea'
Kerria japonica 'Pleniflora'
Lantana camara 'Goldmine'
Lonicera nitida 'Baggesen's Gold'
Mahonia aquifolium 'Apollo'
Mahonia japonica Bealei Group
Mahonia x *media* 'Buckland'
Mahonia x *media* 'Charity'
Mahonia x *media* 'Lionel Fortescue'
Paeonia lutea var. *ludlowii*
Phlomis fruticosa
Phygelius aequalis 'Yellow Trumpet'
Potentilla fruticosa 'Abbotswood'
Potentilla fruticosa 'Goldfinger'
Pyracantha 'Soleil d'Or'
Rhododendron luteum
Rhododendron macabeanum
Ribes sanguineum 'Brocklebankii'
Rosa 'Felicia'

Rosa 'Golden Wedding'
Rosa 'Graham Thomas'
Rosa 'Masquerade'
Rosa 'Peace'
Rosa xanthina 'Canary Bird'
Salix lanata
Salvia officinalis 'Icterina'
Sambucus racemosa 'Plumosa Aurea'
Sambucus racemosa 'Sutherland
    Gold'
Santolina chamaecyparissus var. *nana*
Sophora microphylla 'Sun King'
Spartium junceum
Spiraea japonica 'Golden Princess'
Spiraea japonica 'Goldflame'
Viburnum rhytidophyllum

Climbers

Campsis radicans 'Flamenco'
Celastrus orbiculatus
Clematis 'Bill MacKenzie'
Clematis tangutica
Hedera colchica 'Sulphur Heart'
Hedera helix 'Buttercup'
Hedera helix 'Goldheart'
Hibbertia scandens
Humulus lupulus 'Aureas'
Jasminum officinale 'Fiona Sunrise'
Lonicera japonica 'Halliana'
Lonicera japonica 'Hall's Prolific'
Lonicera x *americana*
Lonicera x *italica* 'Harlequin'

Rhododendron macabeanum

summer onwards. Yellow roses are another popular choice and cultivars to look for include 'Amber Queen' (amber), 'Arthur Bell' (gold), 'Canary Bird' (clear yellow), 'Chinatown' (pink-edged yellow), 'Felicia' (apricot-yellow), 'Golden Wedding' (gold), 'Graham Thomas' (clear yellow), 'Masquerade' (clear yellow), 'Mountbatten' (gold) and 'Peace' (pink-flushed, deep yellow). *Clematis tangutica* and 'Bill MacKenzie' are two of the best yellow-flowered climbers, producing their blooms in succession from mid-summer.

Colour selector: white and green

Green is the predominant colour in most gardens and usually forms the canvas upon which all the other colours are added. However, you can create a garden using greens alone because there is such a wide range of shades and textures.

Atmospheric greens

The amazing variations of the tones of green and its variety of finishes, ranging from matt, through silk to high gloss, means that a real tapestry can be achieved with this colour.

Green also harmonizes with yellows and blues, which lie on each side of it on the colour wheel, so you can safely combine these, creating a calming atmosphere.

Alternatively, you can combine greens with contrasting reds and oranges, which lie opposite the green sector on the colour wheel. Green is an excellent foil for these strong colours, which would otherwise dominate the display.

In spring and summer, *Prostanthera cuneata* produces clusters of broadly tubular, pure white flowers.

Variegated green

Many ornamental shrubs and climbers have attractively variegated leaves: striped, splashed or edged with contrasting shades of green, yellow or white. These are particularly useful for adding light to darker corners and for providing interest all around the garden when other plants are out of season.

Monochrome plantings need a backdrop of green or silver to act as an effective foil, but they can also be used to striking effect in full sun, be eye-catching in dappled shade and glowing in full shade.

White

Like green, the importance of white within the garden palette is often overlooked. It is the universal colour that can be used in conjunction with any other colour in the colour wheel, or on its own.

When backlit in the twilight hours, white flowers can seem almost ghostly, shimmering above the border. Few flowers are pure white all over; most have a hint of green, pink, yellow or blue that makes them even more intriguing, while others may have pure white petals but combine with a contrasting colour, such as a splash of golden stamens. Even the purest of white flowers open from coloured buds that change the whole perception of the display.

There is a huge range of garden-worthy shrubs that bear brilliant white flowers in profusion. Among the best is *Amelanchier lamarckii*, a spectacular shrub in spring when smothered in star-shaped, white flowers accompanied by bronze-tinted emerging leaves. The flowering Chinese dogwood, *Cornus kousa* var. *chinensis*, is even more conspicuous when covered in its creamy-white flower bracts that fade

Choisya ternata

to white before turning red-pink during early summer, followed by strawberry-like fleshy fruit.

The star magnolia, *Magnolia stellata*, is equally dramatic, producing silky buds that open on bare branches in early spring to reveal stunning, lightly scented, white, star-shaped flowers. For sheer visual power, few shrubs can equal the floriferous *Exochorda* x *macrantha* 'The Bride', which produces elegant arching branches smothered in brilliant white flowers during late spring.

Roses should not be overlooked either, including 'Blanche Double de Coubert' (pure white), 'Boule de Neige' (pure white), 'Happy Birthday' (creamy-white), 'Ice Cream' (ivory), 'Iceberg' (pure white), 'Kent' (pure white) and 'Polar Star' (pure white).

Several climbers are noted for their sparkling white flowers. The *Clematis armandii* varieties 'Apple Blossom' and 'Snowdrift' bear their fragrant, star-shaped blooms in early spring against leathery, evergreen leaves. For early summer, *Solanum jasminoides* 'Album' is hard to beat, with its clusters of jasmine-scented flowers and glossy, dark green leaves.

White and green shrubs and climbers to try

Shrubs

Amelanchier lamarckii
Amelanchier x *grandiflora* 'Ballerina'
Brugmansia suaveolens
Buddleja davidii 'White Profusion'
Buxus sempervirens 'Suffruticosa'
Buxus sempervirens 'Elegantissima'
Calluna vulgaris 'Alicia'
Calluna vulgaris 'Spring Cream'
Camellia japonica 'Nobilissima'
Camellia x *williamsii* 'Jury's Yellow'
Carpenteria californica
Chaenomeles speciosa 'Nivalis'
Choisya 'Aztec Pearl'
Choisya 'Goldfingers'
Choisya ternata 'Sundance'
Cistus x *aguilarii* 'Maculatus'
Cistus x *corbariensis*
Clethra alnifolia
Clethra alnifolia 'Paniculata'
Colutea arborescens
Convolvulus cneorum
Cornus 'Eddie's White Wonder'
Cornus kousa var. *chinensis*
Cotoneaster salicifolius 'Gnom'
Cytisus multiflorus
Daboecia cantabrica f. *alba*
Deutzia gracilis
Drimys winteri
Erica carnea 'Springwood White'
Escallonia 'Iveyi'
Eucryphia x *intermedia* 'Rostrevor'
Eucryphia x *nymansensis* 'Nymansay'
Euonymus 'Emerald Gaiety'
Exochorda x *macrantha* 'The Bride'

x *Fatshedera lizei* 'Variegata'
Fatsia japonica 'Variegata'
Garrya elliptica
Gaultheria mucronata 'Wintertime'
Gaultheria procumbens
Griselinia littoralis
Hebe cupressoides 'Boughton Dome'
Hebe pinguifolia 'Pagei'
Helianthemum 'Wisley White'
Hydrangea arborescens 'Annabelle'
Ilex aquifolium 'Silver Queen'
Itea ilicifolia
Lantana camara 'Snow White'
Lavandula angustifolia 'Nana Alba'
Lavandula stoechas 'Snowman'
Ligustrum lucidum 'Excelsum Superbum'
Lonicera fragrantissima
Lonicera x *purpusii* 'Winter Beauty'
Magnolia stellata
Nerium oleander
Olearia ilicifolia
Olearia macrodonta
Olearia x *haastii*
Osmanthus delavayi
Osmanthus x *burkwoodii*
Pachysandra terminalis
Philadelphus 'Beauclerk'
Philadelphus 'Belle Etoile'
Philadelphus x 'Lemoinei'
Philadelphus 'Manteau d'Hermine'
Philadelphus microphyllus
Philadelphus 'Virginal'
Phoenix roebelenii
Phygelius x *rectus* 'Moonraker'
Pieris 'Forest Flame'
Pieris formosa var. *forrestii* 'Wakehurst'
Pieris japonica 'Purity'
Pieris japonica 'Variegata'
Pittosporum 'Garnettii'
Pittosporum tenuifolium 'Variegata'
Potentilla fruiticosa 'Abbotswood'
Rhododendron 'Cunningham's White'
Rosa 'Blanche Double de Coubert'
Rosa 'Boule de Neige'
Rosa 'Happy Birthday'
Rosa 'Ice Cream'
Rosa 'Iceberg'
Rosa 'Kent'
Rosa 'Polar Star'
Rubus 'Benenden'
Ruta graveolens 'Jackman's Blue'
Santolina chamaecyparissus var. *nana*
Sarcococca confusa

Rosa 'Boule de Neige'

Sarcococca hookeriana var. *digyna*
Sarcococca hookeriana var. *humulis*
Spiraea 'Arguta'
Spiraea nipponica 'Snowmound'
Spiraea prunifolia
Spiraea thunbergii 'Albovariegatum'
Syringa vulgaris 'Michael Buchner'
Viburnum davidii
Viburnum tinus 'French White'
Viburnum x *burkwoodii*
Viburnum x *carlesii*

Climbers

Cissus antartica
Cissus rhombifolia
Clematis 'Alba Luxurians'
Clematis armandii 'Snowdrift'
Clematis 'Belle of Woking'
Clematis cirrhosa 'Wisley Cream'
Clematis 'Duchess of Edinburgh'
Clematis florida 'Seiboldii'
Clematis 'Henryi'
Clematis 'Huldine'
Clematis 'Lasurstern'
Clematis 'Marie Boisselot'
Clematis 'Miss Bateman'
Fallopia baldschuanica
Jasminum officinale
Jasminum officinale 'Clotted Cream'
Mandevilla boliviensis
Passiflora caerulea 'Constance Elliot'
Solanum jasminoides 'Album'
Stephanotis floribunda
Trachelospermum jasminoides
Wisteria floribunda 'Alba'
Wisteria sinensis 'Alba'

Philadelphus 'Manteau d'Hermine'

Colour selector: red

Plants with scarlet and vermilion flowers are often seen as the showgirls of the border, demanding attention as they cry out from the chorus of other more subtle shades all around them.

Hot reds

Reds fall on the hot side of the colour wheel, and so sit particularly happily alongside oranges and yellow in fiery combinations. However, reds have much more going for them than that.

The most saturated reds, which fall in the middle of the spectrum, have the most intense colour and can hold their own in any display. However, if they are used too liberally, they will dominate all the other colours surrounding them. For this reason, saturated red flowering plants with large blooms need to be used with care and reserved for creating distinctive points of focus in a border of more subtle shades, such as pale green.

Shrubs with scattered, small red flowers are much easier to accommodate in mixed planting schemes because their effect is moderated by the intermittent

backdrop of foliage that peeks through from behind the vibrantly coloured flowering display.

Velvet-reds

Rich velvet-reds that have just a hint of blue will add sensuality to a planting scheme and are particularly well suited to combining with plants of a purple tone. Many flowers offer plum-purple shades, which are now very popular. More subtle than the saturated reds, velvet-reds tend to add warmth and intimacy to a planting scheme.

Brilliant reds

Shades of red also can be introduced into the border by including plants with purple or red foliage. This can be a seasonal highlight, such as the brilliant red, glossy young leaves of *Photinia x fraseri* 'Red Robin' or, for longer-term display, *Berberis thunbergii* 'Atropurpurea Nana', with its dark purple leaves that turn a brilliant red in autumn, or *Cotinus coggygria* 'Royal Purple', another red-purple-leaved, bushy shrub that turns brilliant scarlet in autumn.

Japanese maples such as 'Atropurpureum', 'Bloodgood' and 'Garnet' make excellent specimens for small gardens, with their attractive palm-like, lobed or deeply cut dark purple leaves that look spectacular all summer before turning brilliant shades of red at the end of the growing season.

Crimson and scarlet

The ever-popular crimson and scarlet roses, such as 'Alec's Red' (crimson), 'Alexander' (vermilion), 'Charles de Mills', 'Fragrant Cloud' (deep-scarlet), 'Ingrid Bergman' (deep red), 'Just Joey' (coppery-red), 'Loving Memory' (dark red), 'Rose de Rescht' (deep mauve-red), 'Royal

Rosa 'Danse du Feu'

William' (deep-crimson), 'Ruby Anniversary' (ruby-red), 'Ruby Wedding' (ruby-red), 'Suffolk' (golden-centred, deep-scarlet) and 'The Times Rose' (dark-crimson), shouldn't be overlooked.

However, there are many other red-flowering shrubs worth considering, including the vermilion-red *Potentilla fruticosa* 'Red Ace', which blooms from late spring to autumn, or the stunning *Paeonia delavayi*, which bears single, cup-shaped, blood-red flowers from spring into early summer.

Red also makes a splash at the end of the growing season as shrubs and climbers take on their autumnal hues. Few sights are more spectacular than the blood-red foliage of the crimson glory vine, *Vitis coignetiae*, when its huge, heart-shaped leaves turn fiery shades, accompanied by bunches of small, blue-black, inedible grapes.

Equally impressive are the deeply divided, slightly puckered green leaves of the Virginia creeper, *Parthenocissus quinquefolia*, which transform in autumn as they take on brilliant shades of crimson and purple. When autumn turns to

Pieris 'Forest Flame'

Red shrubs and climbers to try

Shrubs
Abutilon megapotamicum
Acer palmatum 'Bloodgood'
Acer palmatum 'Fireglow'
Acer palmatum 'Osakazuki'
Acer palmatum 'Sango-kaku'
Acer palmatum var. dissectum
    'Atropurpureum'
Amelanchier lamarckii
Amelanchier x grandiflora 'Ballerina'
Aucuba japonica 'Rozannie'
Aucuba japonica 'Variegata'
Berberis thunbergii 'Atropurpurea Nana'
Berberis thunbergii 'Bagatelle'
Berberis thunbergii 'Dart's Red Lady'
Berberis thunbergii 'Harlequin'
Berberis thunbergii 'Helmond Pillar'
Berberis thunbergii 'Red Chief'
Callistemon citrinus 'Splendens'
Calluna vulgaris 'Dark Star'
Calluna vulgaris 'Wickwar Flame'
Camellia japonica 'Adolphe Audusson'
Camellia japonica 'Mikenjaku'
Camellia x williamsii 'Anticipation'
Ceratostigma griffithii
Chaenomeles x superba 'Crimson and
    Gold'
Chaenomeles x superba 'Nicoline'
Colutea x media 'Copper Beauty'
Cornus 'Eddie's White Wonder'
Cornus alba 'Sibirica'
Cornus alba 'Spaethii'
Cotinus 'Flame'
Cotinus 'Grace'
Cotoneaster dammeri
Cotoneaster frigidus 'Cornubia'
Cotoneaster horizontalis
Cotoneaster 'Hybridus Pendulus'
Cotoneaster salicifolius 'Gnom'

Cytisus 'Boskoop Ruby'
Daboecia cantabrica 'Bicolor'
Desfontainia spinosa
Enkianathus cernuus f. rubens
Erica carnea 'Ann Sparkes'
Erica carnea 'Challenger'
Erica carnea 'December Red'
Erica carnea 'Myretoun Ruby'
Escallonia rubra 'Crimson Spire'
Euonymus europaeus 'Red Cascade'
Fothergilla gardenii
Fuchsia 'Mrs Popple'
Fuchsia 'Pumila'
Fuchsia 'Riccartonii'
Gaultheria mucronata 'Mulberry Wine'
Gaultheria procumbens
Helianthemum 'Ben Heckla'
Helianthemum 'Ben Hope'
Helianthemum 'Henfield Brilliant'
Hibiscus rosa-sinensis 'The President'
Ilex aquifolium 'J.C. van Tol'
Leptospermum scoparium 'Red Damask'
Leucothoe 'Scarletta'
Leycesteria formosa
Paeonia delavayi
Photinia x fraseri 'Red Robin
Potentilla fruticosa 'Red Ace'
Pyracantha 'Saphyr Rouge'
Rhamnus alaternus 'Argenteovariegata'
Rhododendron 'Dopey'
Rhododendron 'Geisha Red'
Rhododendron 'Klondyke'
Rhododendron 'Lord Roberts'
Rhododendron 'Mother's Day'
Rhododendron 'Scarlet Wonder'
Ribes sanguineum 'King Edward VII'
Ribes sanguineum 'Pulborough Scarlet'
Rosa 'Alec's Red'
Rosa 'Alexander'

Viburnum betulifolium

Rosa 'Charles de Mills'
Rosa 'Fragrant Cloud'
Rosa 'Ingrid Bergman'
Rosa 'The Times Rose'
Rosa moyesii 'Geranium'
Skimmia japonica subsp. reevesiana
Virburnum betulifolium
Weigela 'Bristol Ruby'

Climbers
Berberidopsis corallina
Bougainvillea 'Scarlett O'Hara'
Campsis x tagliabuana 'Madame Galen'
Clematis 'Ernest Markham'
Clematis 'Niobe'
Clematis 'Rouge Cardinal'
Clematis 'Ville de Lyon'
Clianthus puniceus
Eccremocarpus scaber
Lonicera x brownii 'Dropmore Scarlet'
Parthenocissus quinquefolia
Parthenocissus tricuspidata 'Robusta'
Vitis 'Brant'
Vitis coignetiae

winter, sparking red stems stand out from the dormant borders, with the red-barked dogwood *Cornus alba* 'Sibirica' taking centre stage with its brilliant red winter stems.

Coral
If you are looking for a shrub that offers year-round interest then seriously consider the coral-bark maple, *Acer palmatum* 'Sango-kaku'.

This magnificent, ever-changing plant offers startling coral-red young shoots that dramatically set off the emerging palm-shaped, orange-yellow leaves in spring. The leaves gradually turn green in summer, before taking on fabulous shades of yellow in autumn. When these lovely leaves eventually fall, they reveal their brilliantly coloured stems throughout the winter.

Clematis reds
Clematis with flowers in shades of red include the semi-double, reddish-purple blooms of *Clematis viticella* 'Purpurea Plena Elegans', which are produced *en masse* from mid-summer onwards, and the ever-popular 'Ville de Lyon', which offers large, cherry-red flowers with contrasting golden centres through the summer and into the autumn.

Colour selector: purple, black and blue

Lying on the cool side of the colour wheel, purple, blue and black are all recessive colours and as such seem to sink back into the border — creating a subdued, almost brooding, edge to the garden atmosphere.

Purple

Despite its apparent richness and associations with opulence, purple is surprisingly calming and soothing. However, it doesn't take to competition all that well and will tend to get lost if it is included in a mixed scheme.

The best way to use purple is in isolated blocks, surrounded by greens and silvers, or combined with bluish-pinks such as lilac. Purples also associate well with cool blues and greens as well as hot reds, which lie either side of the purple sector in the colour wheel. For colour contrast, go for yellow, which lies opposite the purple sector on the colour wheel, or startling whites, which will help lift the mood and provide sensational highlights.

Softer mauves and lavenders are also part of the purple group and are even more subdued than their more vibrant, violet counterparts. They

Vitis vinifera 'Purpurea'

benefit from being used in bold swathes of single colours that lead the eye from one part of the garden to another, such as a lavender hedge alongside a path or a wisteria cascading over a boundary fence.

Black

By contrast, black (actually the darkest shade of purple) can be used for focal point plants when it is dotted within a planting of pale foliage plants. They look even better against a backdrop of silver or intermingled with the purest of whites. In blocks, black is too austere and will get overwhelmed in mixed colour schemes. Good examples of black plants include the lovely *Sambucus nigra* 'Black Lace and *S. nigra* 'Black Beauty.

Blue for illusion

Blue is perhaps the most tranquil colour in the garden palette, associating well with water and seating areas where its peaceful ambience can be best appreciated.

Although one of the least prominent colours, blue is also useful for creating illusions in a small garden where you want to increase the sense of space.

Like purple, blue associates well with white flowers and silver foliage, as these complement its introverted nature. It also harmonizes with other cool colours, such as bluish-purples and bluish-greens — both tones making an ideal antidote to the more flamboyant colour combinations often found elsewhere.

True blue

Pure blue flowers have a wonderfully luminescent quality about them, which means they often look their most spectacular at dusk and dawn, when other dominant colours seem

Cotinus coggygria

to recede and allow the blues to shimmer magnificently.

Perhaps the most reliable and impressive blue flowering shrub is the late spring-blooming Californian lilac (*Ceanothus*). Excellent varieties include: 'Burkwoodii', which bears clouds of sky-blue flowers above a compact evergreen shrub with bright green glossy leaves; 'Concha', which makes a dazzling mound of dark blue flowers; and the relatively new 'Italian Skies', which is covered in dense clusters of brilliant blue flowers. Other blue flowers that should not be forgotten are the popular 'Puget Blue' (dark blue) and 'Trewithen Blue', which bears fragrant, rich blue blooms. For a late show, go for 'Autumnal Blue', which bears clouds of bright blue flowers.

Vivid blue

Other shrubs that produce piercing, vivid blue flowers include the Chinese plumbago *Ceratostigma willmottianum* 'Forest Blue' and the ground-hugging periwinkles *Vinca major* (deep blue) and *Vinca minor* (pale blue). Alternatively, you might like to try *Caryopteris* x *clandonensis*

Purple, black and blue shrubs and climbers to try

Shrubs
Acer palmatum 'Atropurpureum'
Acer palmatum 'Garnet'
Ballota acetabulosa
Berberis thunbergii 'Atropurpurea Nana'
Berberis thunbergii 'Bagatelle'
Berberis thunbergii f. *atropurpurea*
Buddleja davidii 'Black Knight'
Buddleja davidii 'Nanho Blue'
Calluna vulgaris 'Amethyst'
Caryopteris x *clandonensis*
Caryopteris x *clandonensis* 'First Choice'
Ceanothus arboreus 'Trewithen Blue'
Ceanothus 'Autumnal Blue'
Ceanothus 'Burkwoodii'
Ceanothus 'Concha'
Ceanothus impressus 'Puget Blue'
Ceanothus 'Italian Skies'
Ceanothus thyrsiflorus var. *repens*
Ceratostigma griffithii
Ceratostigma willmottianum
Ceratostigma willmottianum 'Forest Blue'
Cistus x *argenteus* 'Peggy Sammons'
Clerodendrum trichotomum var. *fargesii*
Cordyline australis 'Atropurpurea'
Cordyline australis 'Purple Tower'
Cordyline australis Purpurea Group
Cordyline australis 'Red Star'
Cornus alba 'Kesselringii'
Corylus maxima 'Purpurea'
Cotinus 'Grace'
Cotinus coggygria 'Royal Purple'
Daboecia cantabrica 'Atropurpurea'
Fuchsia 'Mrs Popple'
Hibiscus syriacus 'Blue Bird'
Hydrangea macrophylla 'Blue Wave'
Hydrangea macrophylla 'Mariesii'
Hydrangea serrata 'Bluebird'
Hydrangea villosa
Indigofera heterantha
Lavandula angustifolia 'Hidcote'
Lavandula angustifolia 'Lady'
Lavandula angustifolia 'Munstead'
Lavandula angustifolia 'Royal Purple'
Lavandula 'Fathead'
Lavandula 'Helmsdale'

Lavandula stoechas 'Papillon'
Lavandula stoechas 'Rocky Road'
Lavandula x *intermedia* 'Grappenhall'
Lavandula x *intermedia* 'Grosso'
Magnolia 'Susan'
Magnolia x *soulangeana* 'Lennei'
Photinia x *fraseri* 'Birmingham'
Rhododendron 'Blue Danube'
Rhododendron 'Blue Diamond'
Rhododendron 'Blue Peter'
Rhododendron 'Purple Splendour'
Rhododendron 'Sapphire'
Rosa 'Cardinal de Richelieu'
Rosa 'Roseraie de l'Haÿ'
Rosa 'William Lobb'
Rosa rugosa 'Rubra'
Rosmarinus officinalis 'Severn Sea'
Salix hastata 'Wehrhahnii'
Salvia officinalis 'Purpurascens'
Salvia officinalis 'Tricolor'
Sambucus nigra 'Black Beauty'
Sambucus nigra 'Black Lace'
Syringa meyeri var. *spontanea* 'Palibin'
Syringa vulgaris 'Charles Joly'
Tamarix 'Rubra'
Tibouchina urvilleana
Vinca major
Vinca minor
Vinca minor 'Argenteovariegata'
Vinca minor 'Atropurpurea'
Vinca minor f. *alba* 'Gertrude Jekyll'

Climbers
Akebia quinata
Ampelopsis megalophylla
Aristolochia littoralis
Billardiera longiflora
Clematis alpina
Clematis alpina 'Frances Rivis'
Clematis alpina 'Frankie'
Clematis alpina 'Pamela Jackman'
Clematis 'Barbara Jackman'
Clematis 'Comtesse de Bouchaud'
Clematis 'Etoile Violette'
Clematis 'Fireworks'
Clematis 'General Sikorski'

Solanum laciniatum

Clematis 'Jackmanii'
Clematis 'Jackmanii Superba'
Clematis 'Mrs Cholmondeley'
Clematis 'Mrs N.Thompson'
Clematis 'Multi Blue'
Clematis 'Perle d'Azur'
Clematis 'Polish Spirit'
Clematis 'Prince Charles'
Clematis 'The President'
Clematis viticella 'Purpurea Plena
    Elegans'
Clematis 'Vyvyan Pennell'
Cobaea scandens
Lonicera henryi
Lonicera japonica var. *repens*
Lonicera periclymenum 'Belgica'
Parthenocissus henryana
Parthenocissus tricuspidata 'Veitchii'
Passiflora caerulea
Plumbago auriculata
Solanum laciniatum 'Glasnevin'
Sollya heterophylla
Vitis vinifera 'Purpurea'
Wisteria floribunda
Wisteria floribunda 'Royal Purple'
Wisteria sinensis
Wisteria x *formosa*

'Heavenly Blue', for its impressive dark blue flowers, or *Hibiscus syriacus* 'Blue Bird', for its exotic-looking, violet-blue, trumpet-shaped summer blooms, each with a maroon eye.

Blue clematis
Finally, there are a couple of clematis that are worth mentioning in the blue category. These are 'Perle d'Azur', for its beautiful yellow-centred, lilac-blue flowers, produced in succession from mid-summer onwards, and 'Prince Charles', which offers pale mauve-blue flowers with green centres.

Scent selector

Fragrance is an elusive quality that is almost impossibly difficult to define. Not only does each person's perception of scent vary from day to day, but atmospheric conditions, location and the blend of scents in the air all have an impact.

The fragrant garden

Although scent is a bonus to the gardener, its reason for existence is to attract insects for pollination. For this reason, many winter-flowering plants are aromatic. However, there are not many pollinators around at this time of year, so the flowers have to work particularly hard to attract them – and they do.

Some plants throw out their scent with gay abandon, and can be smelled over long distances. Others are much more discreet and can only be appreciated when you get up very close to them. Some are only noticeable during the evening, as the light fades. Generally, a warm, sunny day brings out the scents of shrubs and climbers, but there are some that are much more noticeable during or after a fall of rain.

Summer scent: *Rosa* 'Zéphirine Drouhin'.

Many gardeners believe that modern-day flowers have lost their delicate fragrance when compared to old-fashioned varieties. In a lot of cases, this is true. As breeders develop more and more hybrid plants, particularly roses, for even larger blooms, a wider range of colours and disease resistance, it is sometimes at the expense of their aromatic charms. However, breeders are now aware of this and are taking more care to preserve the other beauty that satisfies the gardener's senses – that of smell.

Fragrance or odour?

It is essential that you check out a plant's fragrance in person before you buy – because one gardener's pleasing fragrance is another gardener's bad odour.

Subtle fragrances are often the worst offenders: it seems the more delicate the scent, the greater the range of reactions it receives, with unusual scents the most likely to be perceived completely differently by different people.

The main reason for this is that a particular fragrance is made up of various layers. The first layer is the ephemeral part of the scent that the nose picks up initially and its influence on the appreciation of the whole scent varies from one person to another. This is the part of the scent that grabs your attention, for good or for bad.

Spring scent: *Viburnum x juddii*

Soon the nose becomes aware of a more representative part of the fragrance, which is the main body of the scent. Then finally, the experience transforms as you appreciate the underlying part of the fragrance that stays with you.

Scent structure

Perhaps the best way to picture the structure of a scent is as a pyramid, as described by the leading French rose breeder, Henri Delbard.

In his pyramid, the top is the 'spirit' of the fragrance and includes the citrus scents and more aromatic elements, such as aniseed and lavender. In the middle is the 'heart' of the scent, which includes floral, fruity, spicy and earthy fragrances. At the bottom is the 'base' scent, which comprises the woody elements. Examples of this are cedar or balsam.

Universal scents

There are some fragrances that are more or less universally liked. Vanilla is a case in point, with the spicy vanilla scent of the chocolate vine (*Akebia quinata*) or the sweet vanilla fragrance of *Clematis* 'Elizabeth' and *C. armandii*, as well as that of wisteria, very widely rated.

By contrast, other sweet scents, such as honey, are loved by some and despised by others. For example, the strong honey scent of most varieties of butterfly bush (*Buddleja*) or that of *Viburnum carlesii* are not universally appreciated, nor is the sweet honey scent of the Californian lilac (*Ceanothus*).

Many floral scents, such as jasmine, honeysuckle and lily-of-the-valley, are also widely acclaimed, as are those with fruity scents such as the peachy scents of *Coronilla glauca*, the fresh pineapple aroma of *Cytissus battanderi*, the spicy orange of

Spartium junceum and the perky lemon of *Eucalyptus citriodora*. Many roses have quite complex aromas, including the bananas-and-oranges smell of *Rosa* 'Bobbie James' and *R.* 'Polyanthus Grandiflorus'; the mix of lemon, peach, apricot and pears of

R. 'Nahema'; or very complex fragrance of mandarin, lemon, hyacinth, lilac, mango and lychee of *R.* 'Chartreuse De Parme'.

Many other climbers and shrubs have aromatic foliage, too, which can be resinous-smelling. Examples

Spring-scented shrubs and climbers to try

Shrubs	
Abeliophyllum distichum	*Syringa vulgaris* 'Charles Joly'
Aloysia triphylla	*Syringa vulgaris* 'Katherine Havemeyer'
Choisya ternata	*Syringa vulgaris* 'Madame Lemoine'
Choisya ternata 'Aztec Pearl'	*Syringa vulgaris* 'Michael Buchner'
Choisya ternata 'Goldfingers'	*Viburnum* x *burkwoodii*
Choisya ternata 'Sundance'	*Viburnum* x *carlcephalum*
Cytisus x *praecox* 'Warminster'	*Viburnum* x *carlesii*
Daphne mezereum	*Viburnum* x *juddii*
Drimys winteri	
Fothergilla gardenii	**Climbers**
Fothergilla major	*Akebia quinata*
Magnolia 'Heaven Scent'	*Clematis armandii* 'Apple Blossom'
Magnolia stellata	*Clematis armandii* 'Snowdrift'
Magnolia stellata 'Rosea'	*Clematis* 'Betty Corning'
Magnolia stellata 'Royal Star'	*Clematis flammula*
Magnolia stellata 'Waterlily'	*Clematis montana* var. *rubens* 'Elizabeth'
Osmanthus delavayi	*Clematis montana* var. *rubens* 'Pink
Pieris formosa var. *forrestii* 'Wakehurst'	Perfection'
Rhododendron luteum	*Clematis montana* var. *rubens* 'Tetrarose'
Skimmia japonica 'Rubella'	*Clematis* 'Mrs Cholmondeley'
Syringa meyeri var. *spontanea* 'Palibin'	*Hoya carnosa*
Syringa pubescens subsp. *microphylla*	*Jasminum polyanthum*
'Superba'	*Stephanotis floribunda*

Spring scent: *Choisya ternata*

Summer scented shrubs and climbers to try

Shrubs
Abelia x grandiflora
Abelia x grandiflora 'Confetti'
Abelia x grandiflora 'Francis Mason'
Abelia x grandiflora 'Goldspot'
Aloysia triphylla
Azara dentate
Brugmansia suaveolens
Buddleja 'Lochinch'
Buddleja alternifolia
Buddleja davidii 'Black Knight'
Buddleja davidii 'Nanho Blue'
Buddleja davidii 'White Profusion'
Buddleja globosa
Carpenteria californica
Carpenteria californica 'Ladhams Variety'
Caryopteris x clandonensis
Ceanothus arboreus 'Trewithen Blue'
Clethra alnifolia
Clethra alnifolia 'Paniculata'
Clethra alnifolia 'Pink Spire'
Clethra alnifolia 'Rosea'
Cytisus battandieri
Cytisus x praecox 'Warminster'
Deutzia gracilis
Escallonia 'Iveyi'
Eucryphia x intermedia 'Rostrevor'
Eucryphia x nymanensis 'Nymansay'
Itea ilicifolia
Jasminum humile 'Revolutum'
Lavandula 'Helmsdale'
Lavandula angustifolia 'Munstead'
Lavandula angustifolia 'Hidcote Pink'
Lavandula angustifolia 'Hidcote'

Lavandula angustifolia 'Lady'
Lavandula angustifolia 'Loddon Pink'
Lavandula angustifolia 'Nana Alba'
Lavandula angustifolia 'Rosea'
Lavandula angustifolia 'Royal Purple'
Lavandula stoechas 'Papillon'
Lavandula stoechas 'Fathead'
Lavandula stoechas 'Kew Red'
Lavandula stoechas 'Rocky Road'
Myrtus communis
Myrtus communis subsp. tarentina
Olearia ilicifolia
Philadelphus 'Beauclerk'
Philadelphus 'Belle Etoile'
Philadelphus 'Manteau d'Hermine'
Pittosporum tenuifolium 'Silver
    Queen'
Rosa 'Alec's Red'
Rosa 'Alexander'
Rosa 'Bantry Bay'
Rosa 'Blanche Double de Coubert'
Rosa 'Blessings'
Rosa 'Boule de Neige'
Rosa 'Buff Beauty'
Rosa 'Cardinal de Richelieu'
Rosa 'Charles de Mills'
Rosa 'Chinatown'
Rosa 'Congratulations'
Rosa 'Cornelia'
Rosa 'Felicia'
Rosa 'Fragrant Cloud'
Rosa 'Happy Anniversary'
Rosa 'Heritage'
Rosa 'Ice Cream'

Rosa 'Ingrid Bergman'
Rosa 'Just Joey'
Rosa 'L.D. Braithwaite'
Rosa 'Louise Odier'
Rosa 'Madame Pierre Oger'
Rosa 'Many Happy Returns'
Rosa 'Mary Rose'
Rosa 'Queen of Denmark'
Rosa 'Rosa de Rescht'
Rosa 'Roseraie de L'Hay'
Rosa 'Royal William'
Rosa 'Ruby Wedding'
Rosa 'Silver Jubilee'
Rosa 'Surrey'
Rosa 'Sussex'
Rosa 'Sweet Dream'
Rosa moyesii 'Geranium'
Rosa rugosa 'Rubra'
Rosa xanthina 'Canary Bird'
Rubus odoratus
Sambucus nigra 'Black Beauty'
Spartium junceum

Climbers
Actinidia kolomikta
Cobaea scandens
Jasminum beesianum
Jasminum officinale
Jasminum officinale 'Clotted Cream'
Jasminum x stephanense
Lonicera japonica 'Halliana'
Lonicera japonica 'Halls Prolific'
Lonicera japonica var. repens
Lonicera periclymenum 'Belgica'
Lonicera periclymenum 'Serotina'
Lonicera x americana
Lonicera x heckrottii 'Goldflame'
Mandevilla x amoena 'Alice du Pont'
Passiflora caerulea 'Constance Elliot'
Rosa 'Alberic Barbier'
Rosa 'Albertine'
Rosa 'Aloha'
Rosa 'Bantry Bay'
Rosa 'Breath of Life'
Rosa 'Climbing Iceberg'
Rosa 'Compassion'
Rosa 'Emily Gray'

Rubus odoratus

Rosa 'Bantry Bay'

include cistus and escallonia; some can be camphorous, such as lavender, perovskia, and eucalyptus; while others are simply pungent, as with rue and ribes.

Siting fragrant plants
Aromatic plants are usually best positioned near places where you sit and relax. This could be in containers on the patio, by garden seats or by windows and doors, so that the scent wafts into the house during a warm day or evening. If you have a table and chairs for outdoor eating in the summer months, you

Lavandula angustifolia

may want to grow shrubs in containers so that you can site them nearby on the patio.

Fragrant foliage

Scent is not limited to the flowers of course, as several plants offer wonderfully aromatic foliage, including many herbs such as thyme, rosemary and bay. And not to be forgotten is the citrus-rich smell of lemon verbena (*Aloysia triphylla*).

In some cases, as with flowers, warmth brings out the fragrance, although in most cases it is necessary to crush the leaves or stems so that their aroma is released.

With scented foliage plants, it is best to site them near to a path so that you can run your fingers through them as you walk.

It is easy to run away with the idea of a fragrant garden. However, caution should be taken when planting, as some scents will vie with each other for attention, overwhelm their companions and not allow you to appreciate their individual fragrances. For this reason, when you are planning your purchases, try to smell your plants before you buy them, as some may not be as scented as you wish. Another reason for trying out scents, either in the garden or the plant nursery, is simply that you may not like the fragrance.

Philadelphus Mahonia

x *media* 'Lionel Fortescue'

Hamamelis mollis

Beds and borders

Shrubs and climbers are the building blocks of the garden, providing a permanent framework that holds the design together in harmony. Try to use them in carefully considered groups rather than dotting them around individually. This will ensure that they provide structure and backbone to the overall design.

Using shrubs in borders

The usual way shrubs are used in the garden is in beds and borders — either in a special, dedicated shrubbery or combined with other types of plants, such as perennials and bulbs.

Shrubs that are being added to an existing display are the easiest to select because you already have a fixed reference point provided by the surrounding plants. You might want to choose a new addition to add height, form, texture or seasonal interest to the existing planting

The secret to planting a beautiful border is to design it with layers of colour and different textures, as well as planting shrubs and climbers that will grow at different heights.

The addition of the vibrant red perennial Maltese Cross (*Lychnis chalcedonica*) makes this combination of foliage shrubs come alive.

scheme, or it could be that you just want a more anonymous border plant to use as a background filler that doesn't upset the display.

New border planting

When planning a new shrub border from scratch, the options are seemingly endless. Unless you have a clear idea of what you want to achieve, you could spend a lot of time trying to make up your mind about the best plan to follow.

First-time planters and old gardening hands alike can be a bit nervous about border design, but a simple and effective method is to use a graduated growing scheme. Select small plants for the front of the border, medium-sized ones in the centre and tall shrubs at the back. This provides a slope effect, allowing the plants to be seen in all their glory.

Garden centres and plant nurseries can be very seductive places. One common pitfall is buying all your favourite shrubs and then trying to fit them into a border plan when you get home. This will inevitably end in disappointment. It is far better to decide what effect you are trying to achieve before you buy the plants and then draw up a list of potential candidates for each position in the border.

Factors that you need to take into account include the heights, spreads and growth rates of the larger specimen shrubs that are to go at the back. Also consider the same factors for the smaller ones that will go near the front. However, try not to over-regiment the border by size as this will look unnatural. As a rule of thumb, don't select any shrub that grows taller than the width of the border.

Next to consider are the foliage colours and textures of the plants on your shortlist. Successful planting is achieved when there is a combining of contrasting elements that provide a dramatic appearance or, conversely, a blend of similar elements that provide a soothing, mellow affect.

Combining plants

Combine evergreen and deciduous varieties in the ratio of about two to one, to give a continuity in the display, and mix different forms and outlines for added interest. Finally, consider the seasonal variations, including flowering periods, changes in foliage, berries, bark and scent.

Good plants to try	
Backbone	Kolkwitzia
Abelia	Lavatera
Berberis	Leycesteria
Callicarpa	Perovskia
Carpenteria	Rubus
Ceanothus	Sambucus
Cotoneaster	Syringa
Deutzia	Tamarix
Erica	
Escallonia	**Dome shapes**
Euonymus	Buxus
Fuchsia	Calluna
Genista	Cotoneaster
Hebe	Daboecia
Helianthemum	Daphne
Hydrangea	Erica
Hypericum	Euonymus
Kerria	Gaultheria
Lavatera	Genista
Lavandula	Hebe
Pachysandra	Helianthemum
Potentilla	Hypericum
Ribes	Lavandula
Skimmia	Potentilla
Spiraea	Santolina
Weigela	Senecio
Fountains	**Spiky plants**
Buddleja	Cordyline
Itea	Phormium
Kerria	Yucca

The design of a bed or border will be largely influenced by the shape and size of the garden as well as the effect you are trying to achieve. Unless you are aiming to create a very formal design, most borders look best with sweeping curves rather than fussy shapes or sharp corners and straight lines.

If there is space, you may allow some of the border to form a peninsula so that part of the garden is hidden from view. This achieves the effect of sub-dividing the design and creating a sense of mystery. However, in smaller gardens it is usually best to keep the centre of the plot uncluttered, either laid to lawn or some form of hard landscaping. The deeper the bed, the more plants it will be able to accommodate, but try to avoid very deep beds over 4m (13ft) as they will be more difficult to maintain. On the other hand, very narrow beds (less than 1m/3ft) limit the scope for planting design.

Layering borders

Most borders can be designed in layers. The back layer should comprise most of the tallest plants: wall shrubs and climbers. It is best to choose plants that will provide an attractive, if somewhat plain, backdrop when out of season, so that they can set off the plants in the foreground to better effect.

If the plants are being used to cover ugly walls, fences or other structures, try to choose ones with evergreen foliage so that the disguise lasts all year round. Back-of-the-border plants shouldn't spread too much, otherwise they will tend to dominate the design. Avoid plants that need a lot of maintenance because pruning, spraying and deadheading will be more difficult to carry out in this area.

The low-growing bright blue flowers and dark foliage of *Lithodora diffusa* combine with *Salix repens* for spectacular ground cover.

The front layer should comprise most of the smallest plants. The job of this layer of planting is to provide a transition from the border to the lawn or path that runs along the front. If you choose the right plants, they can also be used to cover up the shortcomings of more spectacular but short-lived displays provided by plants behind. The middle layer of plants should offer most of the seasonal highlights, with colourful flowers at different times of the year and dramatic autumn colours to sustain the display.

Choose a few taller plants to break the regimented effect and give the design a more natural feel. You may prefer to choose plants that flower together in the most spectacular way, or combine plants that flower at different times to create a longer period of interest.

If space is restricted, try to choose plants that offer at least two seasonal features, as well as plants that flower for weeks or months, rather than days, so that the border can continue looking good for a longer period of time.

The silvery leaves of the shrub *Elaeagnus* 'Quicksilver' provide a beautiful foil for the showy flowers of *Erysimum* 'Bowles' Mauve'.

Using shapes for structure

A border simply made up of layers can be attractive, but often the effect seems to lack impact and contrast. For this reason it a good idea to take some time to consider what role each individual plant is to play in the border so that you can combine them to their best effect.

A few will be focal points that act as anchors to the overall display; other plants will be there to provide a backdrop and act as a foil for the more showy plants. They also help define boundaries and are essential in-between fillers that add structure and are generally restful on the eye. You can only have so many drama queens that provide flower power, eye-catching foliage and colourful berries or winter stems in your border, so don't underestimate the value of the less showy shrubs.

Making shapes

Another factor essential to consider is how all the different shapes of your chosen plants will work with each other, as well as the overall appearance of the border. For example, tall and columnar shapes

draw the eye like living exclamation marks, while low-spreading shapes have the opposite effect. Add a sense of movement and gracefulness to a static border using fountain shapes, such as grasses. Further back, try weeping shapes, which tend to harmonize with their neighbours, or spiky shapes for added drama.

To get an impression of how these different shapes will work together, draw an outline of the plants and then cut them out and move them around as if you were designing a stage set until you achieve a combination that appeals to you.

Use the lists on the previous page and the opposite page to help you decide which plants to try. Bear in mind that the plants will grow and change shape over time, so ensure that you give them enough space to spread and develop their true outline. If you don't want it to spread, choose plants that will take well to being pruned.

Year-round interest

Unless you are trying to create a seasonal splash, try to combine plants to provide interest throughout the year. In a small garden it is particularly important that every plant contributes to the display during more than one season. Also, make the most of available space by under-planting shrubs with ground cover and bulbs that flower at other times.

The easiest way to visualize how these different plants will work together is to make a calendar of the plants and their main periods of interest. Use coloured pencils to indicate when their decorative features are on show so that you can see how the colours combine. You can also check how they overlap to achieve continuity in the display.

When planning your beds and borders, try to include a few plants that will add a bold splash at certain times of the year so that the border

A mix of the pink *Rosa* 'Zéphirine Drouhin', the purple *Clematis* 'Lady Betty Balfour' and the large-leaved *Vitis coignetiae* grow happily together in a border.

Great border design combines plants of different heights, textures and colours together to make a pleasing, unifying whole.

design ebbs and flows with the seasons. Equally, don't overlook the value of evergreens and variegated evergreens, as these will provide reliable winter interest as well as a constant setting for the more flamboyant jewels that sparkle at other times.

Using climbers in borders

Climbers are versatile plants that can be used in all three layers of the border design. At the back, they are a space-saving way of covering walls and fences (*see also* page 60); when planted in the middle, they can be trained over structures to add height to borders (*see* page 64) as well as through established plants (*see* page 66). For the front of the border, there are many climbers that will scramble over the ground between shrubs to provide attractive, weed-suppressing groundcover (*see* page 68). Climbers grown across the ground are also a useful way of disguising eyesores such as manhole covers, immovable rubble and old tree stumps.

Climbers for difficult situations

There are climbers and wall shrubs that can be grown in nearly every position in the garden. They not only take up very little space, but allow you take advantage of vertical surfaces that would otherwise remain bare. Perhaps the most challenging site is a cold and shady wall – many plants that will not mind shade or cold winds will not enjoy the dry soil that is often found next to a wall; particularly if rain-bearing winds are coming from the wrong direction, and if the house eaves are keeping rain off.

Fences are less of a problem because water percolates naturally through the soil under the fence. However, walls do have the advantage that they store warmth from the sun (or from the house) and improve a microclimate for the climbers and wall shrubs attached to them. Walls are also permanent structures and can generally carry a greater weight, which can be an issue over time as the plant matures and grows.

Shrubs and climbers for a cold, shady site must be very tough, able to withstand cold winter winds. If plants receive morning sun, they can also suffer damage during rapid thaws after a frosty night. Shrubs to try for these planting positions include climbing hydrangea (*Hydrangea petiolaris*), *Cotoneaster horizontalis*, *Garrya elliptica*, winter jasmine (*Jasminum nudiflorum*) and firethorn (*Pyracantha*), which are all as tough as old boots and provide valuable seasonal interest. Japanese flowering quince (chaenomeles) will also tolerate these conditions, but it flowers and fruits better in the sun.

Climbers to try include varieties of *Clematis macropetala*, *C. montana*, *C. orientalis* or *C. tangutica*; ivy such as *Hedera colchica* 'Dentata Variegata'; and Virginia creeper (*Parthenocissus henryana*). Vertical surfaces that get some sun can be improved with the planting of climbing and rambler roses such as 'Albertine', 'Madame Alfred Carrière' and 'Maigold', as well as *Schizophragma hydrangeoides* and *Vitis coignetiae*.

Seasonal sensations

Colourful	Hibiscus	Choisya
Acer	Hippophae	Convolvulus
Amelanchier	Magnolia	Elaeagnus
Azalea	Nandina	Escallonia
Berberis	Olearia	Euonymus
Camellia	Paeonia	Fatsia
Chaenomeles	Pieris	Griselinia
Cistus	Pyracantha	Hebe
Cornus	Rhododendron	Mahonia
Cotinus	Rhus	Myrtus
Cytisus	Romneya	Olearia
Enkianthus	Rosa	Osmanthus
Eucryphia		Pachysandra
Exochorda	**Evergreens**	Photinia
Forsythia	Aucuba	Pittosporum
Fothergilla	Azalea	Pyracantha
Genista	Camellia	Rhododendron
Hamamelis	Ceanothus	Skimmia

Hedging and screening

There are a number of shrubs that make excellent hedging plants, and which you choose should depend on how big you want it to grow and the amount of time you want to spend keeping it in shape.

Choosing a hedge

The choice of hedging is far wider than the ubiquitous privet. You can choose from flowering, fragrant and fruiting ones, to dwarf, herb and topiary hedges. However, before you choose a variety that meets your requirements, you can reduce the options available by asking yourself the following three questions:

• Do you want a deciduous or evergreen hedge? Evergreen hedges provide constant cover throughout the year, but are more susceptible to winter cold and some soil-borne diseases. Deciduous hedges offer a changing backdrop and are more wildlife friendly.

Before purchasing plants, bear in mind that deciduous shrubs will drop their leaves in the autumn, so if

privacy is your main consideration for a hedge, you would be better off choosing an evergreen shrub, as they provide good all-year screening.

• Do you want a formal or flowering hedge? Formal hedges provide a neat backdrop and complete privacy, but require regular trimming. Informal flowering hedges require little maintenance, but take up more space and aren't as dense.

• Do you want it to grow quickly? Quick-growing hedges provide privacy in a short period of time but will require more trimming once they have reached the desired height.

You also need to consider whether you want a secure boundary or simply a decorative screen. Hedging plants that make dense growth and are covered in vicious thorns make the best impenetrable boundary hedges, while evergreen hedges are an excellent backdrop for other garden features. Available space will also affect the choice you make. Most hedges occupy a strip at least 60cm (2ft) wide, while a few, including

A formal beech (*Fagus sylvatica*) hedge makes a neat garden boundary. Beech is a slow-growing plant and needs little attention.

beech and privet, can be kept half this width with regular trimming. Also consider that evergreen hedges tend to cast deep shade so that few plants will grow at the base on the shady side.

Wildlife hedges

Hedges can provide nesting and roosting sites for birds, and their flowers and berries are vital food sources for insects and butterflies.

Although all hedges offer some benefit to garden birds and other wildlife, a mixture of deciduous species, such as beech, hawthorn, hazel, holly and hornbeam, would be a good choice. Not only will they provide shelter and safe breeding sites, but if you get the mixture right, the hedge can also offer a year-

Buying hedging

Deciduous hedging plants are usually sold as barerooted plants in bundles, while evergreen varieties are available as young plants in small pots. Even though you can get much larger plants in containers, you will save a lot of money if you buy smaller ones. Such plants, about 30–45cm (12–18in) high, will establish themselves more quickly and soon catch up with the larger versions. Shop around, as prices can vary considerably between suppliers.

Low-growing hedges can be successfully made out of lavender bushes. Here, two rows of lavender border a narrow path. As you brush past, the aroma is intoxicating.

Good pl[...]

Sunny
Acacia dea[...]
Actinidia k[...]
Campsis gr[...]
Carpenteri[...]
Ceanothus[...]
Cytisus bat[...]
Eccremoca[...]
Fremontod[...]
Hibiscus sy[...]
Jasminum [...]
Passiflora [...]
Sollya hete[...]
Wisteria fl[...]

Good plants to try

Evergreen hedges	Deciduous hedges	Flowering hedges	Hedges in shade
Aucuba japonica 'Variegata'	Berberis thunbergii	Camellia x williamsii	Aucuba japonica 'Variegata'
Berberis darwinii	Carpinus betulus	Chaenomeles japonica	Buxus sempervirens
Buxus sempervirens	Chaenomeles japonica	Escallonia rubra var. macrantha	Chaenomeles japonica
Chamaecyparis lawsoniana	Corylus maxima 'Purpurea'	Forsythia x intermedia	Euonymus japonicus
Elaeagnus pungens	Crataegus monogyna	Fuchsia magellanica	Ilex aquifolium
Escallonia rubra var. macrantha	Fagus sylvatica	Hebe pinguifolia	Lonicera nitida
Griselinia littoralis	Forsythia x intermedia	Lavandula	Taxus baccata
Hebe pinguifolia	Fuchsia magellanica	Philadelphus coronarius	Viburnum tinus
Lavandula	Ligustrum ovalifolium	Potentilla fruticosa	
Lonicera nitida	Philadelphus coronarius	Pyracantha rogersiana	**Thorny hedges**
Olearia x haastii	Potentilla fruticosa	Ribes sanguineum	Berberis darwinii
Prunus laurocerasus	Ribes sanguineum	Rosa rugosa	Berberis thunbergii
Pyracantha rogersiana	Rosa rugosa	Weigela florida	Crataegus monogyna
Taxus baccata	Weigela florida		Olearia x haastii
Thuja plicata			Pyracantha rogersiana
Viburnum tinus			

shortages. C[...]
on a shady [...]
challenge of[...]
cooler summ[...]
than will be[...]

Make su[...]
fences and [...]
and repair l[...]
before plan[...]
or wall shr[...]
supporting [...]
this stage. [...]
walls and fe[...]
impoverish[...]
improved b[...]
digging in [...]
organic ma[...]

Making a [...]
Although t[...]
put up trell[...]
for climber[...]
plants even[...]
cover-up, a[...]
use an attr[...]
such as a p[...]
creates the [...]
can then tr[...]
the frame s[...]
maintained[...]
attractive i[...]

round larder of food for birds, butterflies and other beneficial insects looking for sustenance.

Garden dividers
Hedges can also be used to sub-divide a garden or provide a neat edging to beds and borders. Although any type of hedge can be used in a large garden, for small gardens slow-growing, dwarf forms are best, such as the evergreen box, grey-leaved flowering lavender, potentilla, hebe and the red-leaved *Berberis thunbergii* 'Atropurpurea Nana'.

Planting hedges
Often, hedges are expected to thrive when planted in poor soil – or even subsoil dug up during house construction or renovation. Many hedges are planted too close to, or underneath, trees, making it difficult for them to get their fair share of nutrients from the soil as they compete with larger roots.

Preferably, hedges should be planted in spring or autumn when the plants are resting. They can be planted in exactly the same way as

PLANTING HEDGES

1 Start by digging a trench where you wish to plant the hedge. Turn over the soil and dig in some manure or compost.

2 Fix a line taut across the centre of the trench and lay out the plants at regular intervals so they have equal growing space.

3 Remove the plants from their pots and position them in the trench, checking that they are accurately spaced.

4 Fill in the trench, firming the soil around each plant. Water throughly and mulch with well-rotted organic matter.

Pergolas and arches

These structures make stunning garden features when covered in colourful climbers – and also provide the practical benefits of shade and privacy.

Using pergolas and arches

Pergolas and arches can be used in a variety of ways around the garden. Pergolas are ideal for providing a secluded hideaway halfway down the garden, or they can be combined with a sunny patio to create a shady retreat on hot sunny days.

Despite their size, they are also a handy design device for use in smaller gardens, where they can be positioned at an angle in a far corner to help disguise the boundary and create the illusion that the garden is bigger than it really is.

Arches have even more uses. Apart from framing an entrance over a gate or at the start of a garden path, they can also be used to highlight a particular feature, such as a bird bath or urn, to dramatically increase its impact. Similarly, if you have a particularly interesting view from your garden, for example an attractive church steeple, a stream or beautiful countryside, bring it to the attention of visitors by framing with an arch. In a small garden, an arch covered in scented climbers or surrounded by scented plants can be used to create an intimate and intoxicating atmosphere around a garden bench.

Arches are also ideal for linking different elements within a garden together. For example, two borders separated by a path become a single feature with a central point of focus when linked by an arch. If you have an uninspiring straight path in your garden, add interest by spacing several identical arches at intervals. Cover them with the same climber and they will seem as one, like an old-fashioned arbour.

Good plants to try

Rambler roses
'Albéric Barbier'
'Albertine'
'American Pillar'
'Emily Gray'
'Rambling Rector'
'Veilchenblau'

Climbing roses
'Bantry Bay'
'Climbing Iceberg'
'Gloire de Dijon'
'Guinée'
'Madame Alfred Carrière'
'Madame Grégoire Staechelin'
'Mermaid'
'Zéphirine Drouhin' (thornless)

MAKING A HOOP FOR CLIMBERS

1 In early spring, make a series of hoops from pliable hazel (*Corylus avellana*) and push each end firmly into the ground.

2 As you bend the hazel, take care that you do not force the curve too sharply. If you do, the hazel might snap.

3 Tie in the long shoots of the climber (a climbing rose is shown here) along the length of the hoop.

4 The leaves of the plant will turn to face the light and new buds will be produced on the upper edges of the curved stems.

5 The plant will have filled out and produced blooms by mid-summer. Remove some of the older stems and tie in new ones annually.

GROWING CLIMBERS UP A TRIPOD

1 Dig a hole big enough to contain the roots of the climber. Position the plant in front of the tripod, not inside.

2 Fan out the stems of the plant and tie them in to the lowest rungs of the tripod, spreading them out to get an even coverage. Water well.

3 In another season the tripod will be covered in foliage and blooms. The structure will also weather down and look less obvious.

Plants for pergolas and arches

All but the biggest and most vigorous climbers can be used to cover pergolas and arches. However, it should be remembered that although leafy growth overhead will provide shade on sunny days, at other times the area may seem gloomy, and persistent drips falling on you after a rain shower can be a big nuisance.

Some climbers such as honeysuckle should be avoided as they are prone to pests that exude honeydew as they feed, resulting in everything underneath being covered with a sticky coating.

You can create the impression that a pergola is completely covered with climbers by training them up and over the outside edges, but leaving the hidden central portion free. Children will love being able to hide in it. Alternatively, you could grow smaller climbers that just cover the uprights and allow a glimpse inside.

The plants you select are a matter of choice and preference, but you do need to consider when you are most likely to use or view the structure, so that the climber is looking its best at that time. You can also combine

different varieties to double the impact or plant pairs of plants that flower at different times in order to extend the show.

Temporary cover

When you first put up a pergola or arch, you will have to wait several seasons before the climbers provide dense cover. During this interim

period, use quick-growing annual climbers to decorate the structure. Plants you could try include the cup-and-saucer plant (*Cobaea scandens*), sweet peas (*Lathyrus odoratus*) or black-eyed Susan (*Thunbergia alata*). If you have sited your structure in a sheltered spot, have a go with Chilean glory flower (*Eccremocarpus scaber*).

A welcome retreat from the sun is achieved by including the *Vitis vinefera* 'Purpurea' for autumn foliage and decorative fruits and *Clematis montana* for colour in spring and early summer.

Ground cover, edging and banks

Low-growing, well-behaved shrubs and some climbers are ideal for growing under the skirt of larger shrubs and trees to provide a weed-suppressing carpet of attractive foliage and colourful flowers. They are also useful elsewhere in the garden and for planting up problem areas where little else will grow.

What makes good ground cover?

A good ground cover shrub should be easy to look after, have a ground-hugging, uniform habit and should be quick to establish after planting. It should form a dense carpet of foliage over the ground, so there is no space for the weeds to grow. On the other hand, it should not be too invasive otherwise it will become the weed rather than the weed suppressor. Most good ground cover plants are evergreen and have attractive foliage, providing year-round cover, but there are one or two very good deciduous candidates worth considering. Ideally, the ground cover should bear colourful flowers, followed by berries as well as autumn and winter colour – but that's probably asking too much!

Genista lydia

Vinca minor 'Aureovariegata'

There are many shrubs and climbers recommended in books and catalogues for use as ground cover, but few actually make the grade in most situations. Ground cover roses are a good example. Although they do sprawl attractively across the ground and put on an excellent show during early summer, they don't produce enough leaf cover early in the season to smother the first flush of weed growth – and weeding between the thorny stems is a practical impossibility.

Using ground cover plants

While ground cover plants are ideal for filling in the gaps between large shrubs and trees, while providing a carpet of attractive foliage and suppressing weeds, they can also be used in other ways around the garden. Problem areas, such as narrow borders along the side of the house or under windows can be filled with suitable ground cover, as can that difficult-to-plant strip along evergreen hedges, where the soil is dry and there is almost constant shade. Similarly, some ground cover plants are an ideal way of covering awkward banks that would be difficult, if not dangerous, to mow if covered in grass. They can also be used to hide eyesores, such as manhole covers, ugly tree stumps, the footings of dismantled walls and old buildings that are too difficult to remove.

In the centre of the garden, ground cover plants make an easy-care alternative to grass, which can be particularly useful in areas that are well away from the main lawn or even in the front garden. Here, they will be on display, so you will need to choose plants that put on a show.

Planting ground cover

When you use plants as ground cover, plant them closer together than is usually recommended. This will ensure a complete cover more quickly, although it will cost more to achieve. The best time to plant is autumn or spring, so the plants will establish quickly. Ideally, plant through a sheet of landscape fabric into weed-free soil to prevent any new weeds appearing until the plants have carpeted the soil.

Budget ideas

Planting ground cover on any scale requires a great number of plants. As most ground cover plantings use swathes of the same variety, you can save money by propagating your own plants or buying in bulk direct from the grower.

Propagating plants doesn't mean waiting for years to get an effective cover on the ground, as many of the shrubs and climbers recommended here produce quick results if planted slightly closer.

If you know what type of ground cover you want, you could buy a large, well-established plant and divide it into many others. For example a 2-litre (3½ pint) pot of a periwinkle, such as *Vinca minor* 'Gertrude Jekyll', could yield up to five plants, while a 5-litre (9-pint) pot could produce ten new plants. Look for a stock plant that is well established in the pot and which has plenty of shoots and buds.

Other ground cover shrubs and climbers are easier to propagate from cuttings. Evergreen shrubs such as *Euonymus fortunei* 'Emerald 'n' Gold', conifers such as *Juniperus* x *media* 'Pfitzeriana Aurea' and climbers such as *Hedera helix* and its cultivars can all be increased easily in this way.

It is also worth visiting nurseries in your area or going to gardening shows to see if they will supply plants in bulk at a reduced cost. Small plants, known as liners, will be a fraction of the cost of a potted plant from the garden centre and will establish quicker. If you want larger plants, some nurseries will offer these at wholesale prices.

Using climbers as ground cover

Many climbers are as happy scrambling over the ground between shrubs and trees as they are covering walls and fences. If you match the vigour of the climber to the space available, it will also be largely maintenance free – requiring no tying in, pruning or training.

For example, in a large space between trees, a variety of the vigorous *Clematis montana* or a honeysuckle, such as 'Halliana', would be ideal. If the space is more restricted, for example in a shrubbery, then ornamental ivies or a less vigorous large-flowered clematis such as 'Lasurstern' or 'Perle d'Azur' would suit. Between flowering shrubs such as roses, choose a groundcover climber that will flower in early spring before the roses open. This will extend the season of interest. Alternatively, choose a variety in a complementary colour that will bloom at the same time as the roses to create a really stunning floral display.

Climbers are often the best option for covering steep slopes or narrow borders at the base of a wall. The climber can be planted in the most favourable position at the top of the slope or at one end of the wall and allowed to cover the ground with its trailing stems. Ornamental vines such as the Boston ivy (*Parthenocissus tricuspidata* 'Veitchii') will cover slopes with a neat bed of evergreen foliage, while varieties of the alpine clematis look delightful scrambling along the front of a wall.

Good plants to try

Under shrubs
Clematis macropetala (cultivars)
Cotoneaster dammeri
Euonymus fortunei (varieties)
Gaultheria procumbens – acid-loving
Hebe pinguifolia 'Pagei'
Hedera colchica (varieties)
Hedera helix (varieties)
Stephanandra incisa 'Crispa'
Vinca major (varieties)
Vinca minor (varieties)

Under trees
Berberis thunbergii 'Atropurpurea Nana'
Clematis montana (varieties)
Cotoneaster conspicuus 'Coral Beauty'
Cotoneaster salicifolius 'Gnom'
Euonymus fortunei (varieties)
Hedera colchica (varieties)
Hedera helix (varieties)
Hypericum calycinum
Rubus cockburnianus
Santolina chamaecyparissus (varieties)

Over sunny banks
Calluna vulgaris (varieties) – acid-loving
Ceanothus thyrsiflorus 'Repens'
Eccremocarpus scaber
Erica carnea (varieties) – acid-loving
Genista lydia

Hedera colchica (varieties)
Hedera helix (varieties)
Rubus cockburnianus
Santolina chamaecyparissus (varieties)
Tropaeolum tuberosum

Alternative to lawns
Calluna vulgaris (varieties)
Erica carnea (varieties)
Hedera helix (varieties)
Vinca major (varieties)
Vinca minor (varieties)

Hiding eyesores
Clematis macropetala (varieties)
Cotoneaster conspicuus 'Coral Beauty'
Cotoneaster horizontalis
Cotoneaster salicifolia 'Gnom'
Euonymus fortunei (varieties)
Humulus lupulus
Vitis coignetiae

In deep shade
Euonymus fortunei (varieties)
Hedera colchica (varieties)
Hedera helix (varieties)
Lonicera pileata
Pachysandra terminalis
Sarcococca hookeriana var. *humilis*
Vinca major (varieties)

Know your soil

The health of your soil is crucial to the types and quality of the plants you can grow. It is therefore essential that you have some understanding of the type of soil you have, and its advantages and limitations, before you can choose the correct plants for your garden. Once you know the basic facts about your soil, you can also set about improving it.

Identifying your soil

The quickest and easiest way to find out what type of soil you have in your garden is to handle it. Wet a small amount of soil and rub it between your finger and thumb and literally feel its consistency. By wetting the soil you will be able to assess more easily the types of particles it contains.

• **Gritty** If it feels gritty and the particles easily separate, then the soil has a high sand content. Then try rolling a small ball of the soil in the palm of your hand so you can estimate how much sand it contains: the easier the ball falls apart the greater the proportion is sand.

• **Gritty and cohesive** If the sample feels gritty but the particles hold together well, then it contains sand and loam. The ball of soil should hold together when rolled in the palm of the hand, but will break up when rolled into a sausage shape.

• **Gritty and sticky** If it feels gritty but is slightly sticky to the touch, it contains sand and clay particles. If the ball of soil becomes shiny when rubbed and can be rolled into a sausage shape and bent like a horseshoe without cracking or breaking, it contains sand, clay and also loam.

• **Smooth and silky** If the sample feels smooth and silky between finger and thumb and moulds into a ball and a sausage, but breaks when bent into a horseshoe shape, then it contains mainly loam and silt.

• **Sticky and malleable** If it feels sticky to the touch and the ball of soil is shiny and easy to roll into a sausage, but cracks when bent into a ring shape, then it contains mainly clay with some loam.

• **Very sticky** If the sample literally sticks your finger and thumb together and the ball of soil is shiny, easy to roll into a sausage and bend into a ring shape without breaking or cracking, then it contains mainly clay.

Soil types

All soils are made up of the same basic ingredients: sand, loam, clay, silt and organic matter. The proportions of each ingredient will determine the type of soil you have and how good the soil is for growing different plants. Sandy soil contains

Daphne bholua 'Darjeeling' prefers a well drained but not dry soil that is slightly alkaline.

a high proportion of large, irregularly shaped particles that have air spaces between them. This means that water drains freely so they tend to dry out quickly, which is a bonus in spring as they are easier to work and warm up earlier than other soils, but they are a problem in summer when they are more prone to drought during dry spells. Free-draining soils also tend to have essential soil nutrients washed out, known as leaching, leaving the soil impoverished unless given a regular application of fertilizer.

Clay soil contains a high proportion of tiny soil particles that pack very closely together, leaving very few air spaces. This prevents water from draining through the soil so it remains wet for longer. Clay soils are also heavy and sticky, and so very difficult to cultivate. They are easily damaged if walked on when wet, causing compaction of the surface, which just exacerbates the drainage problems. They are also slow to warm up in spring, and so planting has to be delayed. In

Soil type at-a-glance

Gritty to touch	Sticky to touch	Shines when rubbed	Rolls into ball	Rolls into sausage	Bends into ring	What's in your soil
√	x	x	x	x	x	Sand
√	x	x	√	x	x	Sand and loam
√	√	√	√	√	x	Sand, clay and loam
x	√	√	√	√	x	Clay and loam
x	√	√	√	√	√	Clay

Viburnum 'Eve Price' is easy going, but does best on clay or silty soil.

Plants for different soils

Sandy, chalky or alkaline soil	Peaty or acid soil	Clay or silty soil
Ceanothus	Calluna	Abelia
Ceratostigma	Camellia	Alnus
Clematis	Corylopsis	Bergenia
Cytisus	Cryptomeria	Choisya
Daphne	Desfontainia	Corylus
Euonymus	Enkianthus	Crataegus
Euphorbia	Fothergilla	Kerria
Genista	Gaultheria	Laburnum
Hypericum	Halesia	Malus
Ligustrum	Hamamelis	Philadelphus
Mahonia	Kalmia	Potentilla
Rosmarinus	Larix	Pyracantha
Spiraea	Leucothoe	Pyrus
Stachyurus	Pieris	Rhamnus
Weigela	Pinus	Sedum
Wisteria	Rhododendron	Sorbus
	Sarcococca	Symphoricarpos
	Skimmia	Taxus
	Staphylea	Viburnum
		Vinca

summer, clay soils can dry out to form a concrete-hard crust with a distinctive cracked surface as the soil shrinks. Clay soils are usually fertile.

Silty soil contains mainly medium-sized particles, and so tends to drain well in winter but retain soil moisture in summer. It is also usually fertile. Silty soils are easily damaged if walked on when wet, causing a compaction of the surface, known as 'capping'.

Loamy soil contains a mixture of particle sizes and so has the advantages of all the other soils, without the disadvantages. Loamy soils are usually easy to cultivate and have a robust and stable structure that drains well in winter and is still fairly moisture retentive in summer. They also generally warm up quickly in spring and are usually fertile.

Soil-testing laboratories

For really accurate soil analysis you will have to send off a soil sample to a specialist laboratory for testing. Set up for the agricultural and horticultural industries. Some local authorities also offer a soil analysis service for gardeners, for which there may be a nominal charge. Not only will they test your soil accurately for pH, but many will provide an analysis of the main plant nutrients: potassium, phosphate and nitrogen as well as some trace elements (magnesium, calcium, manganese, iron, copper and zinc, for example), and information about the organic matter content. The most comprehensive soil analysis services will give some recommendations for fertilizer and lime application rates in order to improve your soil.

This sort of professional analysis may be worth considering if you have just moved to a new house and don't know anything about the garden's history, or where you've had difficulties in the past and suspect the problem lies in the soil. You can also use this sort of soil analysis to test deliveries of topsoil to make sure they are up to standard, but bear in mind that results can take anything from a week to a month to get the results, so you may have to hold back on planting.

Hamamelis mollis prefers peaty or acid soil.

Assessing your soil

Once you are familiar with your soil type, there are two other key factors you need to find out so that you can take steps to improve the soil before planting: how acid the soil is and which nutrients it contains.

Testing your soil

Although the best way to find out about your soil in detail is to send a representative sample off to a specialist laboratory to have it analysed, you can find this out with reasonable certainty by carrying out a simple set of tests yourself.

There are cheap and reliable soil-testing kits widely available from garden centres and DIY stores that will tell you your soil's pH level as well as indicate the nutrient balance in your soil.

The pH level is a measure of your soil's acidity or alkalinity. Each plant has an ideal pH range in which it will thrive, which varies from plant to plant. To make the most of your plants' growing potential, it is

The rock rose (*Helianthemum*) is a dwarf shrub that is able to thrive on almost any soil that is reasonably fertile and well drained.

essential that you test a soil sample that's representative of the whole area you are planning on planting up. Make sure that you do not test contaminated areas, such as where a compost heap has been, otherwise the results will be invalid.

The easiest and most reliable way to select a representative soil sample is to lay out four canes on the soil surface in a large 'W' shape. Use a hand trowel to dig five small holes about 15cm (6in) deep at the points of the W. Scoop out a little soil from the bottom of each hole and place this in a sieve over a bucket. This will remove stones, pieces of chalk and organic matter that might skew the results. Mix the sieved soil samples together before testing.

Altering acidity

The best range of nutrients are provided when the soil has a pH value of about 6–7. It is possible to temporarily reduce the acidity of the soil by applying lime several weeks before planting. Choose either garden lime or ground chalk that has

been made for the purpose. The amount of lime you apply will be determined by the type of soil and its pH. For example, to change a clay soil from pH5 to pH6 will require about 1,200g of lime per square metre, while you would need only 800g per square metre on loamy soil and 400g per square metre on a sandy soil.

It is essential that you follow the guidance notes on the soil test kit and the instructions on the lime

A more high-tech soil-testing device is an electronic meter. When the probe is inserted in the soil, a reading of its pH level is given.

Checking drainage

Another important factor to establish when planting a new area is how well it drains. If the soil is poorly drained, you may wish to take steps to improve it before planting. To check how well your soil drains, dig several holes about 30cm (12in) deep spaced randomly across the plot. Fill each hole with water and see how quickly it drains. If there is still water in the hole after 24 hours, you may have a drainage problem. This can usually be overcome by digging deeply and incorporating plenty of well-rotted organic matter and grit into the soil, otherwise you will have to consider installing land drains, or building raised beds to improve drainage around the roots of the plants.

packaging to work out exactly how much you need to apply to your soil.

The best time to apply lime is during the autumn or early winter when soil conditions allow. Wear gloves and apply lime only in still, non-windy conditions. Rake the lime roughly into the surface after application. Bear in mind that liming is only a temporary solution, and so you will need to check the soil acidity every few years.

If you intend to add organic matter to your soil before planting, do this during early spring at least two months after liming to prevent the two reacting together and producing ammonia. Use acidic well-rotted farmyard manure on alkaline soil to help lower the pH and alkaline mushroom compost on acid soils to help raise the pH.

Tricky situations

Climbers and wall shrubs are often planted in borders next to walls where the soil is impoverished. In new gardens, the soil can be full of builders' rubble and so needs digging out to a depth of at least 30cm (12in) and replacing with good-quality topsoil from elsewhere in the garden or from a garden supplier. The soil will also be dry because the wall draws water from it via capillary action and, more often than not, prevents rain falling on the border. The best way to counteract this is to add lots of well-rotted organic matter to the soil before planting and to cover the soil surface with an organic mulch afterwards.

In the dappled shade under trees and the dense shade along evergreen hedges, ground cover shrubs can be difficult to establish. Give new plants the best start by planting in spring into well-prepared soil cleared of roots and mulching the soil surface after planting. Pay particular attention to all new plants in difficult situations to make sure they are kept weed-free and well watered through their first growing season.

TESTING YOUR SOIL FOR ITS NUTRIENT VALUES

1 Collect a soil sample from 10cm (4in) below the surface. Take several different samples and mix together for a representative test.

2 Follow the instructions on the kit. Usually, you mix 1 part soil with 5 parts water. Shake well and then allow the water to settle.

3 Using the pipette provided with the kit, draw off some of the settled liquid from the top of the jar.

4 Having drawn off about 5cm (2in) of the solution, transfer the sample to the test chamber in the plastic container.

5 Select a colour-coded capsule (one for each nutrient). Put the powder in the chamber, replace the cap and shake well.

6 After a few minutes, you can compare the colour of the liquid with the shade panel shown on the side of the container.

Planting climbers

Most climbers are planted in the same way as described for shrubs, although the technique varies slightly depending on the type of support they are being grown against. Clematis are the main exception to this rule, since they are planted deeper than other climbers as a precaution against disease (*see* box, page 81).

Planting next to walls and fences

Thorough soil preparation is the key to success when planting next to vertical surfaces, especially if they have foundations. The soil at the base of a wall or fence is usually dry because the border is in the rain shadow of the solid barrier and is often shallow and impoverished. Therefore, it is essential to improve the moisture-holding capacity of the soil by incorporating well-rotted organic matter before planting. Clear all weeds and debris from the soil as you go. If the soil is particularly poor, it may be worth replacing it with fresh soil from elsewhere in the garden or buying it. Also make sure any supporting wires or trellis that is to be attached to the vertical surface is put up before planting (*see* pages 82–83).

You can also aid establishment of the climber by planting it away from the vertical surface so that its roots can spread out in all directions. Dig a hole about 30–45cm (12–18in) away from the wall or fence about twice as wide as the rootball of a container-grown climber. Place the excavated soil on a plastic sheet or old soil bag next to the hole. Unless you are planting a clematis (see below), the hole should be as deep as the container or rootball, so that the specimen will be planted at the same depth as it is in the pot. If necessary, you can check this by standing the pot in the planting hole and laying a bamboo cane across the hole. Remove or replace soil as necessary until the correct planting depth is achieved. Then, fork over

PLANTING A CLIMBER

1 Start by digging a hole twice the size of the rootball. The centre of the plant should be at least 30cm (12in) from the wall.

2 Dig in a generous amount of rotted manure or garden compost. This will help retain moisture around the roots.

3 Put the rootball in the hole, having teased out some of the roots to aid growing. Firm the soil around the plant.

4 Loosen the stems if they have been tied to a cane, spread them out, high and low, and tie them on to the trellis.

5 Water in well and regularly. Climbers need more water as they are usually planted where walls or other plants shield them from rain.

6 Apply a mulch at least 5cm (2in) deep around the plant to help reduce water loss and suppress weeds. Don't pile over the stem.

the bottom of the planting hole. Improve the excavated soil and the soil in the planting hole with well-rotted organic matter and a little bonemeal. Water the climber thoroughly before planting and fill the planting hole with water and allow to drain. Remove the pot and tease out the roots from around the rootball before planting to encourage the roots to spread into the surrounding soil. Place the climber in the centre of the hole and angle it backwards at 45 degrees towards the support. Then backfill the excavated soil around the rootball in layers, carefully firming each layer to remove air pockets. Repeat the process until the hole is filled. After planting, level the surface and then water the climber thoroughly before applying a generous 8cm (3in) deep organic mulch around the plant, but take care not to pile it up against the stem.

Planting next to arches and pergolas

Freestanding supports should be erected and the soil allowed to settle before climbers are planted,

Ideal for growing up supports, *Clematis* 'Jackmanii' is a sun-seeker and will thrive in sunny spots.

Plant clematis deep

Clematis should be planted deeper than other climbers so that the base of their stems are underground. This means making the planting hole about 8cm (3in) deeper than normal. This technique is a precaution against clematis wilt disease, which is a serious problem with clematis – killing all the top-growth. However, any shoots underground are unaffected, so that any deeply planted clematis that suffer from this disease can recover by producing new shoots the following year from healthy buds that form at the base of the stems underground.

following the technique described above. You can plant right next to the support if space is limited, unless foundations were laid under the soil to support the structure. Once planted, untie the climber from its supporting cane in the pot and spread out the stems. Carefully tie them into the support. If there is only one stem, tie the cane into the support and pinch out the tip of the climber to encourage new side shoots to be produced.

Planting near shrubs and trees

Climbers can also be planted alongside established shrubs and trees that can be used as a natural support. The soil is likely to be dry and full of roots, so choose a planting position at the edge of the host plant's canopy, where water will naturally run off when it rains – this is known as the 'drip zone'. Carefully excavate a hole and cut off any fibrous roots that have become exposed. If large roots are in the way, move the planting hole to another position. Improve the soil as before, then line the sides of the planting hole with old pieces of softwood. This will help prevent the surrounding roots from the host plant competing with the climber while it becomes established. In time, the timber will rot away.

Providing support: vertical surfaces

Although some climbers can scramble up, over and through supports without any assistance, all wall shrubs and some climbers require a helping hand. By providing wires, trellis or mesh supports, you can also train the climbers and wall shrubs to go exactly where you want them to grow.

Supporting climbers and wall shrubs

There are a number of ways you can support climbers and wall shrubs up a vertical wall or fence. It is essential that you choose a support that's robust and sufficiently large to match the vigour of the climber or wall shrub. For example, annual sweet peas can be supported on plastic mesh or wire netting loosely anchored to the vertical surface, while a vigorous clematis will need a substantial trellis that's been securely screwed into place. Indeed, some climbers, such as wisteria, can reach tree-like proportions and need a heavy-duty support to match. The support system you choose should

Some climbers can cling to brick, stone or wood by putting out modified roots.

Vigorous clematis varieties are ideal for clothing the walls, particularly if you want to hide eyesores, such as compost bins.

also be in keeping with its surroundings. For example, on a decorative wall, you may prefer to use a series of parallel wires that are invisible to the naked eye from a short distance. On the other hand, a less attractive structure can be camouflaged or enhanced by adding prominent decorative trellis as a support for a new climber.

Using wires

Most climbers and wall shrubs can be supported using wires. Wires are the most versatile support, covering any shape or size of surface. Choose a strong galvanized or plastic-coated wire, say 10 to 14 gauge. The wire needs to be held 5–8cm (2–3in) away from the wall or fence using special wall fixings called vine-eyes. This gap will allow air to flow around the plant and help prevent the wall remaining damp for long periods. There are two types of vine-eye: triangular pegs that are hammered into the mortar between courses, or screw-in eyelets that are

Clinging plants will cover any vertical surface without needing any support, as seen with this *Hydrangea petiolaris*.

secured in holes drilled into the wall and filled with wall plugs. Space parallel wires every 30cm (12in) up the wall for most climbers and wall shrubs, but use a fan-shaped or even vertical arrangement of wires for twining climbers. When training and tying in new growth to the support, make sure that it is in front of the wires, so that it helps to hide the wires, the plants are easy to prune and, if necessary, can be detached and lowered from the wall without removing the support system.

Using trellis

Wooden trellis is available in a range of decorative shapes and sizes, but you can also make your own from inexpensive wooden lathes, which can be bought from builders' merchants. These will have been pressure-treated against rot, so just need to be cut to length and fixed with screws. Making your own trellis won't work out any cheaper than buying ready made, but it can be tailored to fit any size or shape of wall or fence.

All types of trellis need to be attached to battens or wooden blocks on the wall so that the trellis is held 3–4cm (1–1½in) away from the vertical surface. Ready-made trellis may look attractive, but the battens are actually spaced too close together. If you make you own, aim to space them 30cm (12in) apart for most climbers and wall shrubs. Expanding trellis is even worse. It isn't as strong as ready-made panels and is usually more expensive. However, it is easy to transport and can be expanded to fit the space available, so is worth considering for very restricted areas and lightweight climbers.

Ready-made trellis is also useful for extending the height of your boundary fence. Special post extensions are available, or you can make your own using 8cm- (3in-) wide exterior quality plywood. There is a wide range of trellis styles available, from simple squares to a diamond pattern or basket weave, so you can select one to suit your garden design.

Trellis can be used to break up the appearance of large walls and fences, too. For example, eye-catching perspective panels effectively draw the eye to the centre of the trellis and the climber it supports. Alternatively, use strips of standard trellis panels to hide a prominent downpipe or other eyesore or paint decorative trellis as an effective way of disguising ugly walls or fences, or even a garden shed. Choose from a wide range of coloured stains made for the purpose, or make your own by diluting oil-based exterior gloss paint in the colour of your choice with white spirit in the ratio of 1:3.

Using mesh

Plastic-coated wire mesh or plastic mesh panels are also available in a limited range of colours. They are easy to cut to size and can be shaped around doorways or windows, used

GROWING CLIMBERS UP WIRES

1 Drill holes where you want the vine-eyes, which will support the plant, to go. You can hammer them in, but a drill makes it easier.

2 If you are using vine-eyes with a screw fixing, insert a plastic plug into the wall first. Then screw the eye into the plug.

3 If you are using wedge vine-eyes, hammer them into the masonry.

4 Thread the wire through the hole in the vine-eye and then wrap the excess back on itself to keep it taut and secure.

5 Arrange the longest stems to the wire and tie in with plastic ties or string. Ensure that the stems lie flat against the wall.

6 The stems should be fanned so the plant can cover the wall as it grows and produce more buds on the top edges of the stems.

to cover downpipes or to fill in gaps in freestanding structures such as arches.

Like wires and trellis, they will also need supporting away from the wall using vine-eyes or wooden battens. However, mesh is less pleasing on the eye than trellis and plastic mesh isn't strong enough for vigorous climbers.

Access for maintenance

Both the vertical support and the trellis attached to it will need maintenance from time to time. Although most ready-made trellis has been pressure-treated against rot, which should protect it for at least

ten years, the trellis may need repairing every now and then as the staples may become loosened by wind-rock and the weight of the climber pulling on it.

Some climbers can be cut back to near ground level to free the trellis, which can be removed so that the supporting wall or fence can be maintained. With sufficient space and a flexible climber, you might prefer to unscrew the trellis and lay it down on the ground with the climber still attached while you carry out repairs. However, if the wall requires regular maintenance, painting for example, you can make the whole job easier if you attach the

Some climbers hold on by twining up their support as they grow, and so do not require routine tying in through the growing season.

ERECTING A TRELLIS

1 Start by digging a hole at least 60cm (2ft) deep. If your soil is light, you may need to dig an even deeper hole to secure the trellis.

2 Put the post in the hole and partly fill with a dry-mix concrete. Check the upright, adjust if necessary and then continue filling the hole.

3 When you fill the hole with concrete, make sure to ram it down very firmly. Once the concrete has 'cured' it will be solidly secure.

4 Lay the trellis next to the ground to work out where the next hole should be. Dig the next hole as for the first.

5 You now have two posts at the right position for the trellis. Offer up the trellis and nail the panel on to the supporting posts.

6 As you progress putting up the panels, stop and check the uprights regularly, ensuring they are level and at the right angle.

bottom of the trellis panel to the lower batten using galvanized hinges. You can then can lower the top of the panel away from the wall and replace it in exactly the right position in just a few seconds.

Next to doors and windows

Climbers and wall shrubs can look delightful when trained to frame a doorway or window and, as long as you choose the right plants, it is as easy to achieve as growing them against other vertical surfaces.

Aim to choose a plant that will provide year-round interest. This effect can be formal or informal, depending on the type of plant you choose. For example, a small-leaved evergreen could be used to create neat, leafy pillars if they are positioned on either side of the door, while a languid, scrambling clematis or rose can offer garlands of colour and scent throughout the summer months.

Plants to avoid around doors and windows include anything that is very vigorous, because it will need constant cutting back. Also steer clear of thorny climbers and wall shrubs, opting for the spineless varieties instead, as children and unaware visitors could get nasty scratches if they brush against them.

Plants that are prone to being attacked by sap-sucking insects, such as honeysuckle, are also worth avoiding, because the resultant honeydew excreted by such pests will make a mess on your windows, as well as making the ground around a doorway sticky underfoot.

Train your selected plants up the wall to the side of the window or doorway by tying them into a support. To do this, either use strong horizontal wires spaced 30cm (12in) apart up the wall, held taut

A fragrant honeysuckle will take just one or two seasons to clothe supporting trellis. The plant is ideal for growing up structures, as it is not too heavy and spreads well.

between vine-eyes, or install a trellis by screwing it to a series of battens. This will ensure good air circulation between the wall and the plant, helping to prevent disease problems. Make sure the battens are made from pressure-treated timber to prevent rot and that they are fixed with rust-resistant screws. You can either plant the climber or wall shrub straight into the soil at the base of the wall

or you may prefer to set it into a large, permanent container. Before you begin planting, make sure the soil has been improved with well-rotted organic matter and keep the plant well watered until it has become established.

Position the climber or wall shrub at least 18in (45cm) away from either side of the doorway so that there is room for growth.

Providing support: freestanding structures

Climbers can be used to cover vertical structures all around the garden. They are an ideal way of adding height to borders as well as creating living focal points that attract the eye.

Arches and pergolas

Although attractive features in their own right, arches and pergolas can be used to enhance the overall design of the garden: framing an entrance or feature; leading the eye farther down the garden; connecting separate elements within the garden; or creating the illusion of space by emphasizing an attractive view outside the garden. Pergolas are useful for creating secluded seating areas or a shady refuge in a hot sunny garden. Both pergolas and arches can also be used to create covered walkways.

Arches and pergolas are available in a wide range of styles and materials, so there should be one to suit your garden. For example, metal structures look most at home in modern or formal garden settings, while rustic wooden pergolas and

This metal archway provides medium support. The golden hop (*Humulus lupulus* 'Aureus') plant covers the arch with a mass of yellow leaves, which support themselves with curling stems.

arches are perfect for a more relaxed cottage-style garden. For best effect, choose a structure that fits in with its surroundings and select a combination of climbers to suit the position you have in mind as well as the size of the structure. Bear in mind what the structure will look like in winter. An ornate metal structure will tend to stand out and

Creating a living arch

If you have hedges on either side of a pathway, you can create a living arch by training them together. To do this, first select two or three upright growing shoots on the hedging plants adjacent to the path, trimming the rest of the stems back. Insert a 3m (10ft) cane into the ground next to the stems so that they can be trained up vertically. Each year, trim the hedge as usual, leaving the selected stems un-pruned.

When the un-pruned shoots reach about 2.5m (8ft), remove the canes and tie a hoop of wire to the stems on either side of the path, so that the top of the hoop is about the right height for the arch. Then, bend the selected stems over the hoop and tie them in using soft string. If they are long enough to touch at the top of the hoop, tie them together.

Continue to tie in new shoots in subsequent years until the arch is thick enough and the desired shape has been achieved. In following years, keep in shape by regular trimming when you cut back the rest of the hedge. Any type of hedging plant can be trained in this way.

To help climbers get a good coverage, tie in their stems, spreading them out so that they are near horizontal, to encourage flowering.

Repeat-flowering roses are ideal for growing up archways, as they will provide colour and cover for a longer season.

Even when it is not in flower, wisteria makes a good covering for structures because its foliage is abundant even when its characteristically beautiful lavender-coloured drooping blooms are over.

This simple arch is constructed using rustic poles and is covered with variegated ivy.

become a feature in its own right, while one made from wood is likely to blend in more with the rest of your garden.

Metal structures Metal arches and pergolas can be practically maintenance-free if well made. Make sure they are coated completely to prevent corrosion, especially around joints, welds and drilled holes. The structure should seem sturdy and rigid, with strong joints and welds. Have a small tin of matching exterior paint to hand to touch up any chips or unprotected areas after erection to ensure protection.

Wooden structures Most softwood arches and pergolas are pressure-treated to prevent rot, but if you have bought one from a local supplier it's worth checking this before you buy. If the wood was treated before it was cut, then untreated wood will be exposed to the elements and will need painting with preservative before you put the structure together. All wooden arches and pergolas should have strong joints and should not be warped.

Check that the structure is well braced with cross-members so that it will be rigid once put together.

Pergolas and arches are available in kit form, usually flat-packed, and are relatively easy to construct. However, it may require two people to put them together. The key to success is to make sure that the posts are vertical and spaced correctly before securing them and that the crossbars are horizontal. The structure will have to bear the weight of the climbers it supports, which can be considerable after heavy rain. Climber-clad arches and pergolas

Sited in the middle of a wildflower meadow, this wonderfully romantic arch serves no purpose other than to support some roses and provide an absolutely beautiful scene.

A combination of sweet-scented roses, clematis and an overhanging fig makes an intimate, shady area for sitting and relaxing in the summer months.

A newly planted arbour will eventually be smothered in foliage and blooms, creating a tranquil spot for sitting.

also put up a lot of wind resistance when the climbers are in leaf, so check how rigid the structure is before you buy. All types of arches and pergolas need to be well anchored to keep them secure.

Mid-border structures

Simple garden structures such as single posts and tripods are much underrated and under-used. They are ideal for adding instant and inexpensive points of focus to a garden. There are many decorative obelisks now available that look attractive all year round without the need for a climber. Pots and tripods also make effective markers at the ends of paths – acting like sentries to emphasize a change in direction or a meeting point. Posts can also be effective when linked with timber crossbars or wire at the back of the border to provide a backdrop. When festooned with climbers, the simple structure becomes a cascade of colourful flowers and foliage that will add height to your borders and help provide privacy. Making mid-

border plant supports is very straightforward. For example, you can create an attractive obelisk from inexpensive wooden roofing lathes, available from builders' merchants, which come pressure treated against rot. First construct four 2.5m (8ft) high triangular frames that are 45cm (18in) wide at the base, then attach

horizontal battens on each triangle using the same wood, spacing them about 15cm (6in) apart. Fit the four sides together, securing them with weather-proof screws. Finally, add a fence post finial to the top as a finishing touch. You can also make a traditional colonnade out of posts and rope or lengths of plastic chain

A large arbour, built for entertaining, is covered by a variety of climbers, including a purple grapevine (*Vitis vinifera* 'Purpurea'), which needs a strong trellis or pergola to support it.

— an ideal way to make a feature out of your favourite climbing rose. You can also combine trellis with posts within the garden to divide the growing area into separate 'rooms' or to add height to beds and borders. The trellis needn't be a continuous screen — you can create the impression of separate areas using just a couple of matching screens on either side of a pathway and they won't make the garden seem too small or the divisions too claustrophobic. Ornate screens that have been stained in a colour that complements or contrasts with the colour scheme of the surrounding

A secluded spot tucked away in the garden allows you to view your gardening efforts in peace and quiet after a hard day of digging, weeding and pruning.

Growing climbers into established shrubs

Climbers look their most natural when climbing through other shrubs and trees. It is important that you match the vigour of the climber to its host plant and try to choose one that flowers at a different time so that the climber extends the period of interest. The host plant needs to be well established, but not so old that it is no longer growing vigorously.

Position the climber on the side of the prevailing wind so that any gusts will blow the climber as it grows into the host plant rather than away from it. After planting the climber (*see* pages 80–1), hammer a short stake into the ground nearby and attach a rope to the stake. The other end of the rope should be attached to a suitable low branch of the host plant. Untie the climber from its supporting cane, then tie it to the rope, and if the stems are long enough, train them into the canopy of the supporting plant. Do not, as is sometimes recommended, loop the bottom end of the rope under the rootball of the climber when planting, because the climber is likely to be pulled out of the ground by the first strong gust of wind.

plants are the most eye-catching. However, in a small garden you may prefer to give the screen a more neutral or rustic finish so that it is recessive on the eye and blends naturally into the garden. For those who have smaller gardens, siting a mirror surrounded by climbing foliage will give the illusion of more space. Combine this with an arch and the optical effect is one of leading the viewer into another part of the garden, hitherto unseen. A similar effect can be achieved by siting a sculpture at the end of a vista to give a sense of space.

A romantic walkway is created from a series of arches along a path cut through long grass. The arches provide a tunnel effect, leading the eye to the end, where a statue completes the view.

Watering and mulching

Watering is one of the most important and time-consuming tasks around the garden. It makes sense, therefore, to be water-wise and use this increasingly precious resource as efficiently as possible.

Watering efficiently

How often your garden will need watering will be determined by the following factors: the type of plants you have (each plant grows at a different rate); the plant's absorption rate and ability to retain moisture; the site's exposure to sun and wind; the depth and type of mulch you use (if any); the amount of recent rainfall; the amount of hot, drying sunshine; and the amount of organic matter in the soil. Each of these factors will affect how quickly your garden dries out.

Saving water

You can collect your own water to use in your garden. A water butt plumbed into a downpipe off the house or an outbuilding can be in exactly the right place to water climbers and wall shrubs in dry borders alongside. There are many decorative versions now available, some shaped like terracotta pots and urns, so there is no need to hide them away. The butt should also be easy to use. Make sure it is raised so that you can get a watering can or hose to the drainage tap at the base. Choose a butt with a cover to keep the water 'sweet' and clean.

If you live in a hard-water area, saving rainwater is a good idea as it's slightly acidic and so is perfect for watering acid-loving shrubs and climbers grown in ericaceous soil. Waste water from washing or bathing can also be recycled in the garden. Known as 'grey-water', it is suitable for applying to established shrubs and climbers.

Plants lose water through their leaves all the time so it is essential to water regularly to make sure they have enough moisture to replenish the roots, otherwise they will die. Plants growing next to walls and fences tend to dry out more easily and so need extra watering.

That said, most shrubs and climbers do not need regular watering once they are established. However, on well-drained and shallow soils, and elsewhere during drought periods, it is a good idea to water judiciously.

Newly planted shrubs and climbers should be kept well watered throughout their first growing season until they have become well established. You might need to water them for longer if your soil is dry, which is often the case at the base of a wall or on a sunny slope.

Efficient watering

The key to watering efficiently is to water thoroughly when and where it is needed.

Watering a little and often is a common mistake made by novice gardeners. This not only wastes a lot more water through evaporation, but it means that only the surface layer of the soil is moistened. This encourages shallow rooting, which exacerbates the problems you will have during dry spells. Aim to

apply the equivalent of 2.5cm (1in) of water to drought-affected borders. It is best to water during the evening, especially in summer, as this will prevent unnecessary water loss through evaporation caused by the sun drying out the water you have just applied. Also, the hot sun acts like a magnifying glass on the watered leaves and can scorch them.

Rain is slightly acidic, so ericaceous plants like rhododendrons benefit from being watered with rainwater. Collect it in a water butt.

MOVING AN ESTABLISHED SH

1 If possible, root-prune the shrub months before moving to encoura formation of fibrous roots.

3 Dig under the shrub as far as yo may be necessary to cut through a roots that are stubbornly holding i

5 Rock the rootball in the opposit and pull the material through, so completely underneath the plant.

7 Heavier plants require a joint ef pole through the material. With o on each end, lift the shrub out of

Watering systems

Apart from using a watering can, there are several different watering systems available to make the tedious task of watering plants easier.

Perforated hosing This consists of plastic tubing punctured with tiny holes through which the water slowly leaks out. This type of system can be quickly removed when it is no longer needed.

Seep or soak hosing A flexible, porous hose made from rubber is buried in the ground and left in for a season or more.

Drip irrigation This is a system professional growers use. One or more drip nozzles deliver water to individual plants or containers. It can be designed to cover any size and shape of garden.

Sprinklers Although mainly used by gardeners to water their lawns, sprinklers can be very helpful for dowsing beds and borders.

When watering, aim the water directly to the root areas of the plants rather than spreading it liberally all over the garden. You can avoid wetting the surface altogether by sinking a pot or pipe filled with gravel next to the plant and applying the water through this. If the soil surface remains dry, there is the added benefit of fewer weeds to deal with.

Applying a mulch

You can reduce the need for watering still further by applying a loose mulch or laying a proprietary mulch mat. These methods will stop water evaporating out of the soil surface and also help to prevent weed seeds germinating. They are best applied in spring when the soil is moist and also weed-free.

There are two main methods of mulching plants:

Loose mulches These are organic or inorganic mulches, and are the most popular because they not only help to reduce water loss and prevent weed competition, but they also provide food for soil-borne creatures such as ground beetles and earthworms.

These creatures incorporate the humus into the soil and improve its structure and fertility. However, the mulch will need to be topped up each year to remain effective. Aim to apply the mulch of organic matter at a thickness of 5–8cm (2–3in). Use a mulch of well-rotted garden compost, composted bark or cocoa shells and remember to keep topping it up each spring.

Inorganic loose mulches, such as pea gravel and pebbles, also reduce water loss and prevent weeds, but they do not help to feed the soil. On the plus side, however, they look attractive and do not require topping up each spring, so offering an easy-care alternative to organic mulches.

Sheet mulches When you are planting up specimen shrubs and climbers, specially made sheet mulches are an option that is well worth considering.

Also known as mulch matting or landscape fabric, these sheets are all weed-proof. They are more effective weed barriers than loose mulches, but do not look as attractive. However, they can be disguised with a thin layer of soil or mulch if used in a prominent position.

To apply a sheet mulch, lay it over the prepared soil and cut cross-shaped slits in the sheet for the climber to be slotted into. For planted shrubs, place the sheet around the bottom of the plant, surrounding the base of the plant by an area of at least 1 sq m (1 sq yard) of sheeting.

USING DIFFERENT TYPES OF MULCH

1 Bare soil is prone to weeds and loses water through evaporation. Before applying a mulch, remove any weeds in the bed.

2 Avoid using grass clippings as a mulch as they deplete the nitrogen in the soil. They may also root, causing a weed problem.

3 Composted bark is attractive as a mulch. However, don't use fresh bark as it may deplete the soil of nitrogen as it decomposes.

Moving

No matter how good
planning your garden
you may change your
where a shrub or clin
Another reason for n
or climbers is that sc
despite your regular
a plant outgrows its
and threatens to over
other plants. If a pla
welcome, it is time t

The best time to n

Moving established p
work and requires ca
Rootballs will be diff
and heavy to move, s
probably need help.

The best time to r
deciduous plants is d
dormant season (late
early spring). Choose
the soil is not frozen
The transplants will

Once you are happy abou
and enjoy a spectacular d

Pruning climbing and rambling roses

There are hundreds of varieties of
climbing and rambler roses that have
been bred from a wide range of rose
hybrids and species, which means
they vary greatly in how they grow
and when they flower. Before you
can prune your plant successfully,
you really need to know a little
bit about it.

Know your climbing rose

When it comes to climbing roses,
terms such as 'climber', 'rambler'
and 'repeat-flowering' are used very
loosely in nursery catalogues,
gardening magazines and books, so
bear this in mind when deciding
which way you are going to prune

When well cared for and pruned, climbing roses will reward you with spectacular displays of eyecatching – and often deliciously fragrant – blooms.

PRUNING A CLIMBING ROSE

1 When pruning a climbing rose, you can either prune it in situ or untie it, prune it and then tie it back up to the support.

2 Cut out dead and damaged wood and reduce one or two of the oldest stems to a point just above a new shoot.

3 After pruning, tie in the remaining shoots using rose ties or soft garden string. Tie the stems in firmly but not too tightly.

4 To keep your climbing rose tidy, deadhead any faded blooms. Do this by cutting the stem back to a leaf, shoot or bud.

your rose. For this reason, it is
worth taking a little time to get to
know your rose to see how vigorous
it is, where new growth is produced
(from underground, around the base
or part-way up older stems), when it
flowers and whether the blooms are
produced on new growth or stems
produced during previous seasons.
Use the climbing rose checker
(opposite) if you are unsure.

Pruning climbing species roses

Climbing species roses and their
varieties, such as 'Bobbie James',
'Kiftsgate', 'Seagull', 'Wedding Day'
and 'Rambing Rector', are extremely
vigorous roses that need a lot of
space, so they are not really suitable
for most gardens. Sometimes known
as wild roses, they can be trained to
cover a large wall or even left to
scramble through a well-established,
healthy tree. They bloom during
early summer in a single flush,
producing sprays of cream, pink or
white single flowers, often strongly
fragrant. Flowers are borne on stems
produced during previous seasons.
Pruning is a matter of clearing out

dead and damaged stems and thinning out congested growth during early spring. Tie in all stems to their supports.

Pruning rambler roses

Varieties such as 'American Pillar', 'Crimson Shower', 'Dorothy Perkins' and 'Sander's White Rambler', have a single flush of blooms during the summer, which are produced on growth that was formed the previous year. They produce long new shoots from the base. For each vigorous new young shoot, prune out an unproductive old one back to ground level after flowering. Do not prune out an old shoot unless there is a new one to replace it, but remove completely any very old, dead or diseased wood. Also cut back flowered side shoots on the remaining stems to two or three leaves. You can cut out poor-flowering old stems to encourage floriferous new stems. If growth is congested, cut out one old shoot for every new one being produced from the base. Tie in all stems securely to their supports.

Pruning single-flowering climbing roses

This group includes some of the best-loved varieties of climbing roses including 'Albéric Barbier', 'Albertine', 'Gloire de Dijon', 'May Queen', 'Madame Grégoire Staechelin', 'Paul's Scarlet Climber' and 'Veilchenblau', which produce large flowers in a single flush during early summer. Prune after flowering by removing up to one-third of the stems, starting with the oldest. Cut back to near to the base or to a new side shoot produced low down. If there isn't much new growth, cut back older branches to 30–45cm (12–18in) to encourage more next

Climbing rose checker

What is the growth habit of your rose?				
very vigorous	√	√	√	x
flowers once	√	√	√	x
flowers more than once	x	x	x	√
small flowers	√	√	x	x
large flowers	x	x	√	√
flowers on new wood	x	x	x	√
flowers on old wood	√	√	√	x
new shoots from the base	x	√	√	x
new shoots part-way up	√	x	√	√
What you've got:	species rose	rambler rose (single-flowering)	climbing rose	climbing rose (repeat-flowering)

year. Trim back flowered side shoots on the remaining stems to two or three leaves.

Pruning repeat-flowering climbing roses

Flowering on and off all summer long, producing large blooms on new side shoots, these include some of the best value climbing roses such as 'Aloha', 'Bantry Bay', 'Climbing Iceberg', 'Compassion', 'Danse du Feu', 'Dublin Bay' and 'Golden Showers'. Little structural pruning is needed, but they benefit from regular deadheading to encourage further

flushes of flowers. Further pruning is best done in winter, when the weakest and oldest stems can be removed. It is also necessary to cut back flowered side shoots on the remaining stems to two or three leaves. Since these roses tend to put all their energies into flowering after they have become established, rather than extension growth, light pruning and deadheading to remove the faded blooms will encourage further flower production. During the dormant season, dead, damaged or congested growth should be removed completely.

PRUNING CLIMBING ROSES

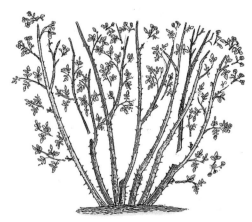

Cut out one or two of the oldest stems to just above a new shoot at the base of once-flowering climbers

PRUNING RAMBLING ROSES

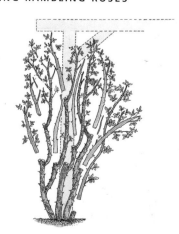

Ramblers are easy to prune. Cut out old stems that have flowered, taking them back to a point where there is a replacement shoot.

Pruning wisteria and honeysuckle

Wisteria and honeysuckle tend to become unruly, tangled masses of stems if they are allowed to grow unchecked. Wisteria need to be pruned twice annually, but honeysuckles can be left for two or three growing seasons before requiring attention.

Pruning and training wisteria

Wisterias are beautiful, dramatic and vigorous climbers that require a lot of space and a very sturdy support – as well as regular pruning – to be seen at their best.

Perhaps the most striking of wall-trained climbers, they're also an excellent choice for growing over a robust archway or pergola and can even be trained as an unusual and eyecatching standard.

Training wisteria

Against walls, wisteria should be trained rather like an espalier fruit tree on strong galvanized or plastic-coated horizontal wires (about 10–14 gauge) and spaced 25–30cm

To ensure successful flowering of wisteria, it needs to be pruned twice a year, in summer and winter. Careful pruning of a wisteria diverts its energies to flower production, rather than the ever-expanding new growth of stems and shoots, and will reward you with a magnificent display.

(10–12in) apart up the wall. The wire needs to be held 5–8cm (2–3in) away from the wall using vine-eyes (see pages 82–3). These allow air to flow around the plant and so help prevent the wall from becoming damp for long periods.

Grow a standard wisteria

Wisteria can also be trained as an eye-catching focal point in the middle of a border. Although spectacular and unusual, it is surprisingly quick and easy to accomplish. After planting, insert a sturdy stake about 15cm (6in) shorter than the eventual height of the desired standard wisteria. Tie in the main shoot to the stake and cut off any side shoots completely. Keep tying in the leader as it grows and removing all side shoots each winter. When the main stem reaches beyond the top of the stake, cut it back to a plump bud. The following winter, select four or five well-spaced side shoots around the top of the main stem to form the head of the standard, then cut out completely all other side shoots lower down the stem. Also cut back the selected side shoots by about one-third – pruning to a healthy bud. Each summer thereafter trim the head of the standard to shape and shorten the side shoots to two or three buds from the main framework.

PRUNING WISTERIA

1 In spring and early summer, wisteria produces long, tendril-like new growth. Cut back leaving 4–6 leaves on each shoot.

2 In early- to mid-winter, cut back summer-pruned shoots even further to about half their length, leaving 2–3 buds on each shoot.

WISTERIA PRUNING CUTS

Cut back the new growth of wisteria each summer to about 4–6 leaves and reduce this even further with a winter pruning.

After planting the wisteria, cut back the main stem to a plump, healthy-looking bud about 90cm (36in) from the ground. Any side shoots should be completely removed. This will encourage new, vigorous side shoots to be produced.

During the first summer, tie in the top side shoot vertically to the horizontal wires to form the new leader. Also tie in the strongest side shoots on either side of the plant at about 45 degrees. Remove all other new side shoots.

During the second winter, untie the two side shoots and lower them to 90 degrees so they can be tied along the first horizontal wire on each side of the plant. Tip-prune the shoots back by about one-third, cutting just beyond a healthy bud. Also, cut the new leader back to a plump, healthy-looking bud about 90cm (36in) above the first tier of branches. Repeat this process until there are sideshoots trained along each of the horizontal wires.

Pruning wisteria

Once the main framework of the plant is complete, wisteria will continue to require pruning twice a year: during late summer and in winter. Any shoots that are required to extend the range or shape of the

wisteria should be left unpruned. The pruning is straightforward: cut back all the whippy new growth to four to six leaves during late summer and, when the leaves have fallen and it easier to see what you are doing, cut the same stumps to just two or three buds from the main framework.

Pruning honeysuckle

Honeysuckles are vigorous twining climbers that can be divided into two groups, according to their pruning requirements. The first group bear their flowers in pairs on wood produced during the current season, for example *Lonicera japonica*. They do not need regular pruning, unless the climber outgrows its allotted space. In this case, cut back all stems during the winter to allow for new growth the following season. Congested specimens can have one in three stems cut back to near ground level, starting with the oldest. The second group, which includes most of the popular varieties such as *Lonicera* x *italica*, *L. periclymenum*, *L. tellmanniana* and *L. tragophylla*, bear their flowers in whorls on stems produced during the previous season. These should be cut back after flowering, pruning out all flowered stems to a newer shoot lower down on the stem.

Aftercare

Pruning inevitably removes part of the climber that provides the plant with energy, so it is a good idea to help the plant recover, especially after severe pruning. Feeding and watering are the most important factors because the climbers will need to put on new growth to replace what it has lost. Choose a balanced fertilizer that contains similar amounts of the main plant nutrients (nitrogen, potassium and phosphorus) as well as other trace elements. Feed in spring after pruning and mulch the ground with a generous layer of well-rotted organic matter to help keep the soil moist and prevent weeds. Water thoroughly during dry spells.

PRUNING HONEYSUCKLE

1 In late winter to early spring, when the stems are bare and you can see what you are doing, cut out any dead and congested stems.

2 Cut just above strong buds. You can be quite brutal when thinning, as honeysuckles are vigorous plants that will thrive on it.

Pruning and training other popular climbers

Provided you match the vigour of a climber to the size of the support and space available, little pruning should be necessary other than the removal of dead or damaged stems and thinning out congested growth. However, a few popular climbers do benefit from more routine pruning.

Climbing hydrangea

The climbing hydrangea, *Hydrangea petiolaris*, needs to be tied into its support until its self-clinging stems get a grip, which may take two or three years. Thereafter, it will climb happily without any help. No routine pruning is necessary unless you want to train the climber to a particular shape, such as around a door frame or keep it on a fan-shaped trellis. Once established, to get the best flowering display, cut back about a quarter of the oldest flowering shoots that grow out horizontally from the support. Do this each year during the winter or early spring. Once the climber has filled its allotted space, it can be kept within bounds by cutting individual stems back to a healthy bud or to their point of origin on the main framework. Overgrown and neglected plants can be rejuvenated by cutting back all stems hard during early spring to the main framework. This is best done over a three-year

Climbers are born to reach for the sky, so make sure you prune them before they do damage to gutters, eaves and roof tiles.

period so that you don't miss out on the flowering display while the climber recovers.

Kolomikta vine

Unless the specimen is already well branched, *Actinidia kolomikta* benefits from being cut back after planting in spring to 30–45cm (12–18in). This encourages side shoots lower down that can then be trained up the support to form the main framework. Space these side shoots about 15cm (6in) apart up the support. During subsequent summers, side shoots can be cut back each year to an outward-facing bud about 15cm (6in) from the framework. In winter, shorten the same shoots to just two buds of the main framework. Once the climber has filled its allotted space, control it by cutting back new growth by about a half its length – cutting individual stems back to a healthy bud or to their point of origin on the main framework. Rejuvenate overgrown and neglected plants by cutting back all stems hard during early spring to the main framework.

REJUVENATING A CLIMBER

1 Climbing plants tend to grow with enthusiasm, criss-crossing their leaves and stems into densely tangled forms.

2 Untangle the old wood and trim away dead and excess shoots until you can see the basic structure of the climber.

3 Cut back the older wood to a strong shoot lower down to encourage strong, vigorous growth from the base.

4 Dead wood or stems that have died back should be cut back to a healthy shoot. This will encourage new growth.

Honeysuckles

Neglected honeysuckles become a huge mass of tangled, spindly, poorly flowering shoots that are prone to pest and disease attack. Often the new growth and the flowers are produced out of sight at the top of the plant. The best way to tackle an overgrown honeysuckle is to give it a hair cut with a pair of shears, removing most of the tangled top-growth. Then, when you can see the framework of stems underneath, identify which of the younger and vigorous stems you want to keep for a balanced shape and remove the rest. Alternatively, you can cut all the stems back to younger side shoots or plump pairs of buds about 30cm (12in) from the ground, but you will miss out on the flowering display for a year or two.

If neglected, honeysuckles will tend to become a tangled mess of stems with their flowers out of sight at the top of the plant.

Passion flower

Varieties of passion flower (*Passiflora caerulea*) all require careful training and pruning to get the best results. These evergreen or semi-evergreen tendril climbers are woody stemmed. The aim with pruning is to develop a permanent framework of branches that will produce a succession of flowering side shoots. If training against a flat surface such as a wall or fence, choose a plant with several stems that can be spaced about 15cm (6in) apart across the support. Unbranched specimens can be encouraged to produce side shoots by cutting back to 30–45cm (12–18in) after planting. If you are training the plant up the post of a pergola or arch, two or three stems will be sufficient. Tie in the stems until they reach the top of the support and then pinch out the growing tip to encourage the side shoots to grow.

On pergolas and arches, trim back all side shoots except those near the top, which can be trained over the support until the framework is completely covered, then simply cut back shoots that have flowered and fruited to two buds of the main framework. Overgrown and neglected plants can be rejuvenated by cutting back one or two of the older branches in the framework each year, to a younger side shoot lower down.

Actinidia kolomikta

Solanum crispum 'Glasnevin'

Potato vine

Solanum crispum 'Glasnevin' and the white form, *S. laxum* 'Album', which have just one or two stems, benefit from being cut back after planting in spring to encourage side shoots to be produced lower down which can then be trained up the support to form the main framework.

These should be spaced out and tied into the support as they grow. Once the climber is established, simply prune all the new growth to just two or three buds of the main framework during late spring after the threat of frost has passed.

Overgrown and neglected plants can be rejuvenated by cutting back one or two of the older branches in the framework each year.

Trumpet vine

Encourage *Campsis radicans* to bush out and produce new shoots from low down on the climber by pruning back to buds about 15cm (6in) from the ground during the spring

after planting. If more than three or four side shoots are produced, remove the weakest first, before spreading out the rest and tying them into their support to form the main framework. Thereafter, once the climber is established, simply prune all new growth to two or three buds of the main framework during late winter or early spring. Overgrown and neglected plants can be rejuvenated by cutting back all stems hard in the winter.

Ornamental vines

Vigorous ornamental vines, such as *Vitis coignetiae* and *V. vinifera*, require very little routine pruning, other than the removal of any damaged or dead stems. If they outgrow their allotted space, cut back about half of the oldest shoots to the main framework and trim the remainder to keep them within bounds. Where space is very restricted, cut all new growth back to within two or three buds of the main framework each winter.

Ampelopsis

An increasingly popular climber, *Ampelopsis brevipedunculata* is a vigorous self-clinging plant that can be left to its own devices if you have the space. In a smaller garden it makes a lovely climber over a pergola, where it can be trained to produce a curtain of handsome leaves and attractive berries. Train the main stem along the pergola cross beam and allow the new shoots to cascade. Cut back all new growth to this framework each winter to keep it neat.

Chocolate vine

One of the 'must-have' plants of recent years, the chocolate vine (*Akebia quinata*) bears maroon-chocolate flowers with a hint of vanilla during late spring and early summer. Although regular pruning is not necessary, if they do need cutting back, do it in late spring after flowering – cutting back with shears to encourage fresh growth. Old plants can be rejuvenated by cutting back one or two of the oldest stems.

Dutchman's pipe

Easy to keep within bounds, the Dutchman's pipe (*Aristolochia*) responds well to hard pruning. If there is no need to keep it within bounds, let its twining stems spread freely. Prune either after flowering during summer or before buds break in early spring.

Coral plant

Do not hard-prune the coral plant, *Berberidopsis corallina*, because it does not respond well to severe treatment. Instead, tidy it up by regular trimming to keep it within bounds. Prune in spring after the threat of frost has passed, removing only dead, damaged or wayward stems.

PRUNING ESTABLISHED CLIMBERS

1 Late autumn or early winter are the ideal times to prune overgrown deciduous climbers. Without the leaves, you can see the shape.

2 The first task is to remove all the dead and damaged wood so that you can regain a good shape and form to the climber.

3 Cut dead wood back to the healthy shoot or, if congested, take it back even farther, but always towards a shoot.

4 Once you have cut out the dead wood, take away congested wood, preferably the weakest and oldest growth.

5 Select some of the strongest and healthiest growths. These are most likely to be the youngest growth. Train them up the structure.

6 Tie in the healthy shoots to the supporting structure using garden twine. Distribute the younger shoots throughout the structure.

Virginia creeper

When the rampant growth of Virginia creeper, *Parthenocissus quinquefolia*, reaches the guttering or the roof, it is time to prune back hard to keep it under control. It climbs up surfaces by using its adhesive tendrils, so you may have to pull it away from its supporting structure to prune it. When established, this creeper can send out new growth up to 6m (20ft) in a year. Plants are very tolerant of trimming and can be cut right back to the base if required to rejuvenate the plant. Any pruning is best carried out in the spring.

Virginia creeper (*Parthenocissus quinquefolia*)

Pruning overgrown shrubs and climbers

If left unpruned for many years, most climbers will become woody and ugly at the base, with most of the ornamental flowers and leaves out of sight at the top of the plant; while shrubs, even if performing well, may simply become too big. Fortunately, many plants respond well to hard pruning and can be given a new lease of life.

Getting started

Renovation pruning is best carried out during the dormant season when the sap is flowing slowly and there are no leaves in the way.

Choose a dry, mild day and arm yourself with a pair of secateurs (pruners), loppers for thicker stems and a pruning saw for woody growth over 3cm (1¼in) in diameter. A pruning knife is also useful for tidying up large cuts and if you are tackling thorny plants, wear stout gloves and goggles to protect your hands and eyes.

Clematis

You can leave clematis unpruned for a few years, but if neglected for longer periods, it will gradually become a mass of unproductive woody stems at the base, with few flowers and little leaf cover. Any flowers that are produced tend to appear right at the top of the plant.

Clematis have a reputation for being difficult to prune (*see* pages 114–15), but they all respond well to hard pruning. Clematis that flower on shoots produced during the current season respond to pruning back very severely to within 30cm (12in) of the base – cutting back to a newer side shoot or a pair of plump, healthy buds. Those that flower on older wood can also be cut back as severely, but you will miss out on the flowering display for a

HOW TO PRUNE OVERGROWN SHRUBS AND CLIMBERS

1 Tangled, congested stems need cutting out to encourage new, more vigorous and free-flowing growth.

2 Cut out the dead wood and take away congested growth, preferably the weakest and oldest, to allow new stems to flourish.

year or two. For this reason, you may prefer to cut them back over a three-year period, removing one in three of the stems during early spring, starting with the oldest.

Roses

Climbing and rambler roses will become less productive if they are left unpruned for many years. Large climbing roses can reach almost tree-like proportions, with large, gnarled, woody bases and sparse leaf cover, with all the green growth and flowers high up on the plant. They will have lost their vigour and often be plagued with diseases during the summer months. Fortunately, all but the most aged of climbing roses can be successfully renovated by severe pruning carried out during the early spring. When the stems are clear of leaves, it is easier to plan where to make the pruning cuts to maintain some sort of balanced shape. Aim to cut out one in three of the oldest stems – either right back to the base or to a younger side shoot close to the ground. Repeat over a three-year period to reinvigorate the plant.

Rambler roses are treated differently as they readily produce new shoots from underground or

very low down on the plant. This means that if they are neglected over a period of time, they will form an impenetrable thicket of stems that gradually lose their vigour. Improve flowering and reduce the overall size of the plant by cutting all the older stems right back to ground level during the dormant season.

Honeysuckles

Neglected honeysuckles can quickly become a huge mass of tangled, spindly, poorly flowering shoots, and they will be more prone to pest and disease attack when they are in this state. As for the blooms, the new growth and the flowers tend to be produced out of sight at the top of the plant.

The best way to tackle honeysuckle is to give it a haircut with a pair of shears, removing most of the tangled top growth. When you can see the framework of stems, identify which of the younger and vigorous stems you want to keep for a balanced shape and remove the rest.

You can cut all the stems back to younger side shoots or plump pairs of buds about 30cm (12in) from the ground, but you will miss out on the flowering display for a year or so.

Pruning neglected shrubs

Vigorous shrubs can soon outgrow their space and will need trimming on a regular basis. If you haven't been able to carry out pruning for some years, you'll need to know which respond well to severe pruning and those best discarded.

Abelia
Responds well to severe pruning. Cut all the stems back to near ground level during early spring.

Artemisia
Responds well to severe pruning, so cut all the stems back to near ground level after the last frost in mid-spring.

Aucuba
Spotted laurels that have got too large or bare at the base can be cut back hard in spring. Remove one in three stems, starting with the oldest.

Berberis
Protect yourself with gloves and goggles before cutting back hard in early spring.

Buddleja
Responds well to severe pruning, so cut all the stems back to near ground level during early spring.

Camellia
Cut back oldest stems to a stubby framework 50cm (20in) from the ground after flowering in spring.

Ceanothus
Evergreen varieties are best replaced, but deciduous varieties can be cut back hard during spring.

Chaenomeles
Flowering quince can be cut back hard in spring after flowering. Remove one in three stems, starting with the oldest.

Choisya
Responds well to severe pruning, so cut all the stems back to near ground level during spring, after flowering.

Cistus
These do not respond well to severe pruning and so are best replaced.

Cornus
Dogwoods grown for stems and leaves can be cut back hard during early spring.

Corylus
Hazels respond well to severe pruning, so cut all the stems back to near ground level during winter.

Cotinus
Cut back to a stubby framework 50cm (20in) from the ground.

Cotoneaster
Fishbone cotoneaster (C. horizontalis) does not respond well to severe pruning, but individual shoots can be removed back to the main stem. Others can be cut back hard during spring.

Elaeagnus
Responds well to severe pruning, so cut all the stems back to near ground level during spring.

Escallonia
Responds well to hard pruning, so cut all the stems back to the main framework during spring.

Forsythia
Plants that are too large or bare at the base can be cut back hard in spring. Remove one in three stems, starting with the oldest.

Fuchsia
Hardy varieties respond well to severe pruning, so cut all the stems back to near ground level during early spring.

Garrya
Responds well to pruning over a period of three years, so cut one-third of the oldest stems back to the main framework each year during spring.

Hamamelis
These can struggle after hard pruning, with the more vigorous rootstock throwing up new shoots. Cut back during spring over three or four years and remove any new shoots from beneath the graft.

Helianthemum
These are short lived plants and are best replaced.

Kerria
Responds well to severe pruning, so cut all the stems back to near ground level during early spring.

Kolkwitzia
Responds well to severe pruning. Cut old stems to near ground level after spring flowering, leaving the youngest stems intact.

Lavandula
Trim after the last frost in mid-spring, but don't cut back into bare wood.

Lavatera
Responds well to severe pruning. Cut stems back to near ground level during early spring.

Leycesteria
Responds well to hard pruning, so cut all the stems back to withing a few centimetres of the ground during spring.

Magnolia
Cut back oldest stems to 50cm (20in) from the ground after spring flowering.

Mahonia
Responds well to hard pruning, so cut all the old stems back to near ground level after flowering in spring, leaving the youngest to replace them.

Olearia
Responds well to severe pruning, so cut all the stems back to near ground level after flowering.

Osmanthus
Responds well to severe pruning, so cut all the stems back to near ground level after flowering.

Philadelphus
Mock oranges can be cut back hard by removing the oldest stems to ground level and cutting the youngest back by about half.

Photinia
Severe pruning is fine, so cut the stems back to near ground level during spring.

Pieris
Cut back oldest stems to 50cm (20in) from the ground after spring flowering.

Potentilla
Cut back hard to a stubby framework, but old plants are best replaced.

Rosmarinus
Cut back all stems by half or replace with a new one.

Sambucus
Can be cut back hard, but best replaced.

Santolina
Cut back hard to a stubby framework, or replace old plants with new ones.

Skimmia
Cut back hard to a stubby framework, but old plants are best replaced.

Weigela
Responds well to severe pruning, so cut all the stems back to near ground level during early spring.

Sowing seed

For successful plants, it is essential to provide the right conditions at the earliest possible moment – and that means when sowing.

Basic methods

How you sow your seed will depend on how many plants you are trying to raise. If you want a lot of shrubs for a hedge or are planning to run a charity stall at your local fair, you may be better off sowing into a prepared seedbed outside during the autumn, provided your soil is well drained.

You will need to protect the bed from birds and rodents. You also need to be prepared to protect early emerging seedlings during early spring with a floating mulch of garden fleece. Alternatively, sow medium quantities of seed in a coldframe, where they are easier to

look after and protect. Many shrubs and climbers will germinate and grow on more quickly if raised indoors, and all tender and borderline plants should be protected in this way.

Large seed can be sown individually during autumn in holes about 10cm (4in) apart, deep enough so that they are covered with about 1–2cm (½in) of soil.

Smaller seed is best left until late winter, when it should be scattered over the surface and lightly raked into the soil or covered in a thin layer of sharp sand. Very fine seed is best sown in spring on the surface and misted regularly to keep moist.

Small amounts of seed and all fine seed are easier to sow in pots or trays filled with potting mix and placed in the coldframe. Most spring-sown seed need a temperature of 15°C (60°F) to germinate and should be

sown in a container in a thermostatically controlled propagator or covered with plastic and placed on capillary matting in a heated greenhouse.

Once the seeds reach sufficent growth, they need to be thinned and potted on, a process called pricking out. This may be the first spring after an autumn sowing or during the following autumn, depending on how the seedlings are developing. Spring-sown seed should be pricked out into individual pots when large enough to handle.

All seedlings need a well-lit spot, out of direct sunlight, and need to be kept moist. All seed raised indoors or in a coldframe will need weaning off the warmer and more protected environment very gradually before planting outside, known as 'hardening off'.

SOWING SEED IN A POT

1 You will need a clean pot, sowing mix, seeds (your own or from a packet), plastic sheeting or a glass cover, a leveller and labels.

2 Fill the pot with the sowing mix. This mix should have few nutrients, which could damage the little seedlings.

3 When the pot is full, level it off and then firm it down, either with a wooden block or the bottom of another pot.

4 Sprinkle the seeds over the top of the sowing mix very thinly. Very small seeds can be mixed with fine sand to make this easier.

5 Spread a fine layer of sowing mix or vermiculite over the surface of the pot. You can use a sifter to do this.

6 Label and lightly water them carefully. Cover with the plastic or glass. Keep inside or place in a heated propagator.

Shrubs and climbers to raise from collected seed

Abutilon Collect dry seed from seed-pods and sow immediately. No treatment necessary.

Amelanchier Pick ripe berries, remove seed and sow immediately. A warm and cold period is necessary for germination; alternatively, sow in spring.

Aucuba Pick ripe berries, remove seed and sow immediately. No treatment necessary.

Berberis Harvest ripe berries and sow after cold treatment to break dormancy; alternatively, leave outside during winter in a coldframe.

Callicarpa Collect seed from ripe fruits and sow immediately in a coldframe outside; alternatively, keep seed until spring and sow then.

Callistemon Collect seed and keep dry until spring. Sow on the surface of the potting mix.

Camellia Seed should be pre-soaked in warm water and its hard covering should be filed down to leave a thin covering. It usually germinates in 1–3 months at 23°c. Prick out into pots when they are large enough to handle. Grow them on in light shade in the greenhouse for at least their first winter.

Caryopteris Collect fruits and remove seed. Keep dry until spring and sow then. No treatment necessary.

Ceanothus Collect seed and soak in hot water before sowing to help break down the hard seed coat. Give cold treatment to break dormancy.

Chaenomeles Collect seed from ripe fruits and sow immediately in a coldframe outside, or keep seed to sow in spring.

Clematis Harvest seed and sow after cold treatment to break dormancy; alternatively, leave outside over winter in a coldframe.

Clianthus Collect dry seed from seed-pods and rub the seed coat or soak in water to break it down.

Leycesteria formosa

Colutea Collect dry seed from seed-pods and rub the seed coat or soak in water to break it down.

Cotinus Collect ripe seed and sow immediately outside or in a coldframe.

Cotoneaster Pick ripe berries, crush and remove seed. A warm and cold period is necessary for germination. Sow in spring.

Cytisus Collect seed and sow immediately outside or in a coldframe. Or store dry until spring, then soak in hot water before sowing to break down the hard seed coat.

Daphne Collect ripe fruit, remove seed and sow immediately after cold treatment to break dormancy. Some species may require two cold winters to germinate.

Enkianthus Surface-sow seed on lime-free potting mix immediately after collection and place in a heated propagator set at 15°C (60°F). Cover seed tray with clear film (plastic wrap) to prevent the seed from drying out.

Euonymus Collect ripe seed and sow immediately outside or in a coldframe.

Fatsia Collect ripe fruits and remove seed before sowing immediately. Place in a heated propagator set at 15°C (60°F).

Forsythia Harvest seed and sow after cold treatment to break dormancy, or leave outside during winter in a coldframe

Fuchsia Collect ripe fruits and remove seed and store for sowing in spring. Place in a heated propagator set at 20°C (68°F).

Genista Collect seed-pods and store dry until spring. Remove seed and sow after

rubbing or soaking in hot water to break down the hard seed coat.

Hibiscus Collect seed-pods and store dry until spring. Extract seed and sow. No treatment necessary.

Hypericum Collect seed-pods and store dry until spring. Extract seed and sow. No treatment necessary.

Kalmia Surface-sow seed on lime-free soil mix immediately after collection and place in a heated propagator set at 15°C (60°F). Cover seed tray with clear film to prevent the seed from drying out.

Lavandula Collect and dry seedheads, remove seed and give cold treatment before sowing to break dormancy.

Leycesteria Collect ripe seed and sow immediately outside or in a coldframe.

Lonicera Harvest ripe berries, remove seed and sow after cold treatment to break dormancy; alternatively, leave outside during winter in a coldframe.

Paeonia Sow after two periods of cold treatment to break dormancy; alternatively, leave outside during winter in a coldframe for two years.

Philadelphus Collect ripe seed and sow after cold treatment to break dormancy; alternatively, leave outside during winter in a coldframe.

Pieris Surface-sow seed on lime-free compost immediately after collection and place in a heated propagator set at 15°C (60°F). Cover seed tray with clear film to prevent seed from drying out.

Euonymus elatus 'Compactus'

Propagating from cuttings

Most shrubs and climbers can be propagated from cuttings. Many will root perfectly well from softwood cuttings, which are taken in spring when the plant is actively growing, but some will root better during the summer from material that has started to ripen at the base, or even in winter from fully ripened wood.

Taking softwood cuttings

Softwood cuttings are cut from new sappy growth taken from shrubs and climbers that are still in active growth. This is usually in mid- to late spring. Collect material while it is turgid and showing no signs of wilting – ideally choose an overcast day or collect early in the morning. Select healthy-looking material that shows no signs of pest or disease attack and is representative of the plant you are trying to propagate. Ideally, choose material that is not flowering or about to flower.

If this is not possible, remove any flowering stems from the material before trimming it into cuttings. When you remove the material from the parent plant, use a clean, sharp knife or pair of secateurs (pruners), cutting just above a leaf joint. Make a clean cut, which will help minimize the chance of infection, and then place the material directly into a labelled plastic bag to prevent them from wilting. You must keep the cuttings out of direct sunlight until you are ready to prepare them.

Prepare the cuttings

• Trim the stems using a clean sharp knife just below a leaf joint, so that the cuttings are 2.5–8cm (1–3in) long, depending on the type of growth that the plant produces.
• Remove the lowest pair of leaves from all the cuttings and the growing tip from longer cuttings. Most cuttings should then have two to four leaves.
• Dip the bottom cut end of the cuttings into a pot of hormone

TAKING ROSE CUTTINGS

1 Select a side shoot that is still green but beginning to turn woody at the base. Cut just above an outward-facing bud.

2 From the removed stem, trim an individual cutting from the base, making the cut just below a leaf joint.

3 Having made your lower cut, now trim back the soft tip to leave a length of stem about 10cm (4in) long.

4 Remove the lower leaves and thorns of the cutting and dip the base in hormone rooting powder. Tap off any excess.

5 Using a dibble or a pencil, make a hole in the rooting medium and put the cutting into it, inserting it to two-thirds of its length.

6 Label the cutting and cover with a plastic bag 'tent' to ensure moisture retention. Don't allow the bag to touch the cutting.

POTTING UP AND POTTING ON CUTTINGS

1 Pot up the cuttings as soon as they have formed strong growth. Use an 8–10cm (3–4in) pot and a potting mix suitable for the young plants. Water thoroughly and keep out of direct sunlight for a couple of days while they recover from the root disturbance.

2 Cuttings that rooted earlier and have already been potted up for a month or more may need moving into larger pots. Check that the roots have filled the compost (soil mix) before you transfer them. If the compost has lots of white roots, pot on into a larger size.

3 When potting on, use a container a couple of sizes larger and put some compost in the bottom. Put the unpotted plant into the new container and trickle the same type of compost around the root ball. Firm well to remove air pockets.

rooting compound (also available as a gel), shaking off any excess, before inserting the prepared cuttings around the edge of a pot filled with moist, fresh cuttings compost.

• It is important to prevent softwood cuttings from wilting, so cover the container with a plastic bag, but make sure it is held clear of the cuttings by inserting short sticks or hoops of wire to hold it proud of

the cutting. Secure the bag in position around the pot using an elastic band. Alternatively, you can place the uncovered pot in a propagator with a lid.

• Place the pots of prepared cuttings in a warm, well-lit position that is out of direct sunlight. When the cuttings show signs of healthy growth, puncture the plastic bags to allow some air to enter and

surround the plant, or open the vents if they are being raised in a propagator.

• Gradually harden off the rooted cuttings by increasing ventilation and lowering the temperature. Once hardened off, they can be planted up individually into larger containers and filled with fresh, moist potting compost (soil mix) (*see* Potting on cuttings steps, above).

Avoiding disease problems

Softwood cuttings and the foliage of semi-ripe cuttings are susceptible to rot before the cuttings have had a chance to root. Apart from choosing healthy cuttings material, ensure that the propagation tools and equipment are clean and the compost fresh and sterile. You can help to prevent disease outbreaks by drenching the cuttings in a fungicidal solution once they are prepared. Check the information on the packaging for dilution rates and whether the fungicide can be used in conjunction with hormone rooting preparations.

ENCOURAGING BUSHY PLANTS

1 Bushy shrubs, such as the fuschia shown here, usually respond well to early 'pruning'. As soon as the cuttings have three pairs of leaves, pinch out the growing tip if you want a bushy shape.

2 New shoots will form after a few weeks. For really bushy plants, pinch out the tips of the side shoots as well. Repeat this process several times throughout the spring to encourage bushiness.

Autumn and winter cuttings

Many deciduous and a few evergreen shrubs can be propagated from hardwood cuttings using stems produced during the most recent season's growth. A few difficult-to-propagate shrubs can be increased from root cuttings taken during the dormant season.

Harwood cuttings

Once the current season's shoots have ripened fully and the leaves have fallen, it is an ideal time to take hardwood cuttings from many clump-forming deciduous shrubs. Select vigorous and healthy stems that are about the thickness of a pencil and typical of the plant you are trying to propagate. Remove the stems from the parent plant using secateurs (pruners), just above a bud. Trim the cutting to about 20–30cm (8–12in) with a straight cut just below a bud at the base and a sloping cut just above a bud at the top. This will help you identify which way up to insert the cuttings later on. Wound difficult-to-root subjects and dip the straight-cut ends in rooting hormone (*see* box, right).

Hardwood cuttings are usually easy to root, but you will have to be patient as it can take up to a year. The simplest way to root them is in a slit trench 15–20cm (6–8in) deep that's been lined with sharp sand. Space the cuttings 8–10cm (3–4in) apart along the row, inserting each cutting into the sand so that about one-third is still above ground when the trench is refilled. Water and weed the area around the cutting throughout the following year and plant out the rooted cuttings or pot them up the following autumn.

Difficult-to-root subjects, such as this *Rhododendron* 'Loder's White', can be encouraged to root by cutting a thin sliver off the base of the stem of the prepared hardwood cutting.

Improving your chances of success

Some shrubs and climbers can be reluctant to root from softwood, semi-ripe and hardwood cuttings, but you can improve your chances of success with many by increasing the size of the cut and applying a specially formulated hormone to the cut surface.

Wounding Difficult-to-root subjects, such as rhododendrons and magnolias, can be encouraged to root by cutting a thin sliver off the base of the stem of the prepared cutting. Use a sharp knife on one side of the cutting a few centimetres (1in) from the base to remove a thin piece of material.

Rooting hormone Rooting hormone products are available as powders, liquids and gels that are simply applied to the base of the prepared cutting before it is inserted into the compost. They contain special chemicals that stimulate rooting, making difficult-to-root subjects easier to propagate and getting quicker results for most other cuttings. To avoid contaminating the hormone, tip a small amount into a saucer and use this. Throw away any unused rooting hormone that's left in the saucer once all cuttings have been completed. Bear in mind that rooting hormone deteriorates rapidly, so buy fresh stocks each year to make sure of its effectiveness.

Root cuttings

A few shrubs, including aralia, chaenomeles, clerodendron, rhus, romneya and rubus, can be increased from root cuttings taken during the dormant season. Excavate around the base of one side of the shrub to expose a few suitable large, fleshy roots. Select vigorous, healthy roots of about drinking-straw thickness if possible and sever them from the parent plant. Prepare the cuttings using a sharp knife so that they are

TAKING HARDWOOD CUTTINGS

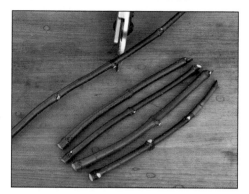

1 Select healthy, blemish-free pieces of wood about the thickness of a pencil. Cut each of these into sections about 20–25cm (8–10in long), angling the top cut.

2 Moisten the bases of the cuttings in water and then dip them in hormone rooting powder. Although not essential, the powder should increase the success rate.

3 Prepare a narrow slit-trench deep enough for the cuttings. Dig down enough so that the top 2.5–5cm (1–2in) of the cuttings will be proud of the earth surface.

4 Loosely fill the trench to about two-thirds with sharp sand or fine grit. This allows the passage of air around the bases of the cuttings and will help prevent rotting off.

5 Insert the cuttings about 8–10cm (3–4in) apart, making sure that the angled cut is uppermost, leaving about 5–10cm (2–4in) above the ground.

6 Firm the soil around the cuttings, ensuring that they are not over-compacted. Leave the cuttings for a whole growing season before lifting and planting out the next winter.

about 5–10cm (2–4in) long, making a straight cut nearest the end of the root nearest the crown and a sloping cut at the other end.

Dip the cuttings in a fungicidal solution to prevent rot setting in. Then, either insert the cuttings around the edge of a pot filled with a well-drained sowing compost (soil mix), with the straight cut just proud of the surface, or lay the cuttings horizontally on a tray of compost.

Cover the compost surface in either case with a thin layer of grit before watering well and allowing to drain. Place the prepared cuttings in a cool, sheltered spot, such as a cold frame or under a cloche in the garden.

Cornus kousa cuttings are taken in the dormant season after the leaves fall in autumn. However, it can be more successfully propagated by using seed, as this produces more vigorous plants.

Layering

Layering is perhaps the most underrated – and yet one of the easiest and most successful – methods of propagating many shrubs and climbers. There are several variations on a theme to layering, all of which involve wounding and partially covering a vigorous, healthy shoot to encourage it to root while it is still attached to the parent plant.

Layering explained

Some plants, notably magnolia and cornus, are very difficult to propagate by taking cuttings. Fortunately, layering is a very simple way of making new plants from old

ones. It involves promoting the development of new roots from a plant's stem, with the stem still attached to the plant. Once it has rooted, it is then severed from the main plant and planted up on its own. Layering can occur spontaneously, when branches of a plant touch the ground and decide to take root.

As the technique of layering is an asexual one, the plants that are produced always have the same flowers, foliage and fruit as the parent plant, which is very beneficial if you want to keep an old and favourite plant going. There are six different methods of layering:

Which method suits which shrub or climber

Simple layering *Abelia, Aucuba, Azalea, Camellia, Carpenteria, Choisya, Hamamelis, Magnolia, Rhododendron, Syringa* and *Viburnum.*
Serpentine layering *Clematis, Lonicera, Magnolia, Rhododendron, Viburnum* and *Wisteria.*
French layering *Acer, Chimonanthus, Cornus, Corylopsis, Corylus, Cotinus, Fothergilla* and *Hydrangea.*
Tip layering *Rubus* and *Jasminum*
Mound layering *Amelanchier, Calluna, Cotinus, Daboecia, Erica* and *Pernettya.*
Air layering *Hamamelis, Magnolia, Rhododendron* and *Wisteria.*

LAYERING

1 Dig over the soil where you want to make the layer, incorporating some well rotted manure or compost.

2 Select a low stem and trim off side shoots Bend it down until it touches the ground. Make a small slit in the stem at that point.

3 Make a hole 10cm (4in) deep, and lay the stem in it, securing in place with a loop of wire. Cover with soil.

4 Additional security can be provided by placing a rock over the buried layer to prevent the stem from moving.

5 Approximately 16–18 months after layering, the shoot will have rooted. Cut it off from the parent plant, making a clean cut.

6 You should now have an independent plant with its own root system. Pot up and grow on until it is big enough to be planted out.

many centuries ago, is a useful way of layering woody shrubs and climbers that don't produce pliable stems near to the ground that can be layered by other more conventional techniques. The best time to air layer is during the spring when new growth starts and sap rises.

Choose a healthy and vigorous stem that is representative of the plant as a whole. Trim off all its side shoots for about 30cm (12in) from the tip. Using a sharp knife, make a clean, shallow cut that is slanting upwards, towards the tip. The cut

should be about 5cm (2in) long and reach about halfway through the stem. Use a matchstick to hold the cut open while you dust both the cut surfaces with a hormone rooting compound.

Next, slide in a little moist sphagnum moss, peat or fresh cuttings compost into the cut before removing the matchstick. Tie a piece of black plastic around them, about 5cm (2in) below the cut, so that it can form a sleeve over the layer. Pack the plastic sleeve with moist sphagnum moss so that it forms a

5–8cm- (2–3in-) diameter bulge around the cut stem. Secure the tip end of the moss or the cuttings compost ball by tying the other end of the plastic to the stem and sealing it with tape. This will prevent any water running down the stem and waterlogging the moss or compost. It is important to use black plastic, rather than the clear type, because it will exclude any light and encourage rooting, while keeping the moss/compost moist but not too wet.

Inspect the layer every few months to see if it has rooted. The time this takes varies from plant to plant and with the time of year – taking anything from just three to 18 months. If there are insufficient roots, recover it after moistening, if required. Leave it for another period before inspecting again.

Once sufficient roots have formed, use a pair of secateurs (pruners) to sever the stem just below the roots. Remove the plastic and carefully tease out the roots before potting up into a container, using fresh potting mix. Don't forget to give it a good drink of water afterwards and to keep it well watered until well established.

AIR LAYERING

1 Layer the plant above the bare area of the stem, just below the leaves. If you are using the technique on a multi-stemmed plant to increase stock, remove a few leaves from the point where you want to make the cut.

2 Carefully make an upward slit about 3cm (1in) long, below the leaf joint. Use a sharp knife, particularly on woody plants, to get a clean cut. Do not cut more than halfway through the stem or the shoot may break.

3 Make a sleeve out of a sheet of black plastic, wrapping it around the stem (clear plastic is shown here to make the process easier to see) Fix the bottom of the sleeve using a twist tie or waterproof adhesive tape.

4 Brush a small amount of rooting hormone (either powder or gel) into the wound to speed up the rooting process. Pack a bit of spagnum moss into the wound to keep it open, or just use a matchstick.

5 Pack plenty of damp spagnum moss around the stem to enclose the wound. Cover with the plastic and secure at the top, as before. Keep the moss moist and check for rooting after a few months.

Common problems

Once well established and growing vigorously, shrubs and climbers will shrug off most pest and disease attacks. However, if they have recently been planted or are not growing well, they can fall victim to a wide range of problems. The most common pests to affect the ornamental garden are slugs and snails, aphids, whiteflies, caterpillars and vine weevils, while the most common diseases are blackspot, mildew, grey mould and rust. With the exception of blackspot, which attacks only roses, all the others can attack a wide range of garden plants.

Whether you want to take any steps to prevent and control pests and diseases on ornamental plants is largely a matter of personal choice. Some gardeners like to maintain a balance between pests and their natural predators, allowing a constant, low level of problems so that there is always sufficient food for the predators to keep them in the garden. Alternatively, you may prefer setting aside an area of the garden for this purpose – a wild corner where you can cultivate plants that are loved by common pests to act as a living larder for predatory birds and insects. You can also encourage natural predators to stay in your garden by providing them with shelter and suitable places to breed.

No matter how good a gardener you are, insects and diseases will affect your plants at some time. The best way to fight them is to understand what these invaders are and how they affect the plants.

Diagnosing problems

Most common pests and diseases are possible to diagnose from the tell-tale symptoms they cause. Use the following guide to help you identify the problem affecting the plants in your garden.

Identifying the problem

A pest is any living creature that causes damage to garden plants. Some are highly visible and easily recognized, while others can be microscopically small and therefore very difficult to spot and identify.

Recognizing that a pest or disease exists is the first stage in learning how to eradicate or control it. The damage created by insects can be infuriating, particularly if you are a gardener who has put many hours of work into the garden in order to enjoy watching your plants blossom and thrive.

Once you establish which plants are being attacked, you are on the way to recognizing the conditions in which the pests thrive. When this happens, you can take steps to remove them. However, many insects look similar, even though the damage they create can vary dramatically. Learning to recognize a beneficial insect from a pest is important. However, it is not just pests that attack plants. Other fungal conditions can develop in plants and stunt or ruin their growth. Bacteria is another important problem group. However, they are never seen and usually function within a plant's tissue. Many can be beneficial, and play an important role in breaking down dead plant material in order to return valuable nutrients to the soil. Most gardeners manage to control or live with a host of pests and diseases, but being able to produce strong and healthy plants is what gardening is all about.

The greyish-white spores of powdery mildew cover the leaves, making it look like a coating of powder. The problem is usually associated with humid air and root dryness.

Black spot is the most common fungal disease of roses. It causes the rose to become lacking in vigour. It can be identified by the round brownish-black spots with ragged margins.

Rhododendron leafhoppers have distinctive reddish markings on their backs. They suck sap from the leaves and cause little harm, but it is thought they contribute to bud blast.

Capsid bugs damage leaves at the shoot tips. They suck sap and also secrete a toxic saliva that kills plant cells. Forsythias, fuchias, roses and hydrangeas are susceptible.

The distinctive pink pustules of coral spot indicate that this troublesome fungus has entered the plant through small wounds, usually caused by careless pruning.

These disfiguring masses are known as galls and they commonly affect forsythia plants. Cut back the affected growth, pruning to ground level. A good recovery should result.

Identifying common problems

LEAF SYMPTOMS

Are there spots on the leaves?
- Silver spots on privet = privet thrip
- White powdery covering = powdery mildew
- Dark green/brown scabby patches = pyracantha scab
- Grey or brown circular spots = fungal leaf spot
- Black spots with yellow edges on roses = blackspot
- Orange spots on leaf undersides = rust
- Transparent spots on roses = rose slugworm
- Yellow spots on rhododendron = rhododendron lacebug
- Translucent patches, often with darker spots = leaf miner

Are the leaves discoloured?
- Yellow leaves, brown spotting = chlorosis
- Yellow patches between veins = magnesium deficiency
- Pale green small leaves = nitrogen deficiency
- Purple small leaves = phosphorus deficiency
- Brown leaf edges = potash deficiency
- Pale green patches between the veins = manganese deficiency
- Furry white covering = downy mildew
- Silvery-grey sheen = silver leaf
- Discoloured leaves, wilt and die = eelworm

Are there holes in leaves?
- Semicircular cuts in leaf edges = leaf-cutter bee
- Small holes = shothole canker

Leaf-cutting bees take neat pieces from leaves, which they use to build their nests.

- Holes and notches = vine weevil
- Ragged holes with evidence of slime trails = slugs and snails

Are there misshapened leaves?
- Rough, often coloured lumps = galls
- Leaf surface grazed off on willow = willow leaf beetle
- Thick leaves, yellow margins = bay sucker
- Tightly rolled leaves on roses = leaf rolling sawfly
- Rolled or webbed leaves = caterpillars
- Distorted leaf clusters on box = box sucker

Are there insects on the leaves?
- Green, black, pink or brown insects = aphids
- White insects on rhododendron = rhododendron whitefly

Have variegated leaves turned green?
- Variegated leaves turn green = reversion

FLOWER SYMPTOMS

Were no flowers produced?
- No flowers = growing conditions (*see* pages 90–7)
- No flowers – incorrect pruning (*see* pages 98–107)

Did the flowers fail to open?
- Flowers fail to open and fall in early spring = frost damage
- Flower buds dry and harden on rhododendron = rhododendron leaf hopper
- White or brown fuzz on withered flowers = grey mould (botrytis)
- Withered flowers = blossom wilt

Are the flowers distorted?
- Flowers open unevenly = capsid bug

Are the flowers discoloured?
- Petal blight

Are there holes in the flowers?
- Holes at the base of flowers = bumble bee
- Irregular holes = moth caterpillars
- Ragged holes = earwigs

Whiteflies suck the sap of the plant and excrete honeydew.

Are the flowers covered in insects?
- Green, black, pink or brown insects = aphids
- Shiny black insects = pollen beetles

Did the flowers disappear?
- Flower buds scattered under plant = birds, squirrels and other wildlife

STEM AND TRUNK SYMPTOMS

Have stems and shoots wilted and died?
- Shoots wilt and die on clematis = clematis wilt
- Shoot tips dying back slowly = die-back
- Shoot tips dying back from flowers = fireblight

Are the stems broad and flattened?
- Flattened stems or flowers = fasciation

Are there spots or lumps on stems?
- Brown spots on bark = scale insects
- Pink or red spots on bark = coral spot
- Rough lumps on forsythia stems = gall
- Rough lumps on stems = crown gall
- Rough patches, sometimes concentric rings on bark = canker
- Unusually flat patches of bark = bacterial canker

Has the bark been stripped?
- Bark removed from right around the trunk = squirrels or rabbits
- Wood stems removed, leaving ragged edge = deer

Is the whole plant distorted?
- Stunted and distorted growth = virus

Dealing with pests

The most common pests in most gardens are slugs and snails, but they do not cause any serious damage to shrubs and climbers once they are established and so are not covered here.

Catch them early

If a prominent or prized plant is attacked, you may prefer to take action to prevent the problem from spreading further. If you catch it early, you simply have to prune out the disease-affected parts of the plant or pick off individual pests, but if the problem becomes established, you may have to sacrifice affected plants to help protect their neighbours – either by cutting the affected plants back hard or removing them altogether. If you grow a lot of one plant in the same area, such as in a rose bed, pest and disease outbreaks are usually worse because the problem can spread easily from one plant to another. You can avoid this by mixing up plants in

Aphids appear quickly and in legions. They suck the sap out of the plants and spread viruses, causing plants to lose vigour or die.

borders or, in the case of roses, growing disease-resistant varieties. However, the following pests are all worth watching out for.

Aphids

Green, black, pink or brown insects attack actively growing shoot tips, quickly forming large colonies. Like other sap-sucking insects, aphids can transmit debilitating virus diseases. Be vigilant and pick off small colonies as soon as they are noticed. Where this is not possible, use a jet of water from a hose to dislodge them. Otherwise, control with a suitable systemic insecticide.

Caterpillars

Voracious eaters of fresh new leaves, several common moth caterpillars can attack a wide range of ornamental plants. Caterpillars of the Angle Shades moth are green with V-shaped markings; Buff-Tip caterpillars are black and yellow; and grey-green caterpillars indicate that you have got the Small Ermine moth in residence. However, if silk webbing can be seen, you might have caterpillars of the web-forming Lackey moth or Hawthorn Webber moth. Fortunately, you don't need to identify the caterpillars to get rid of them. Simply pick off any that you

Caterpillars attack a wide range of plants. Pick them off leaves, let their natural predators deal with them, or use a pesticide.

The evidence of slugs and snails, which eat their way through stems. They are particularly troublesome during wet weather in spring.

see before they do too much damage. Those that produce webbing should have their 'tents' cut from the plant and opened out for birds. Severe infestations can be controlled using a biological control containing the bacterium *Bacillus thuringiensis*.

Vine weevil

Vine weevils seem to attack anything and everything. They can be a significant problem for anyone who grows a lot of shrubs and climbers in containers. Watch out for the tell-tale sign of notched leaves, which indicate the adult female is about, but it is the white grubs up to 8mm (⅜in) long that cause the real damage – feeding unnoticed on the roots. Vine weevils are flightless and so move around quite slowly. They

---

Mammals

Mice, rabbits and deer can all be troublesome in some gardens. Although they are not widespread pests, where they do occur they can cause serious damage to shrubs and climbers. Mice are mainly a problem with new plants and seedlings; rabbits eat young shoots and strip bark from shrubs; while deer will cause similar damage higher up the plant. The best way to deal with mice is to set traps around vulnerable plants, such as in the coldframe or greenhouse. For rabbits, you'll need to erect a boundary barrier at least 90cm (3ft) high, with a further 30cm (12in) buried under the ground; while deer will require a fence at least 1.8m (6ft) high to keep them out of your garden.

are usually introduced to an unaffected garden on new plants. Since vine weevils reproduce parthenogenically, it takes just a single female weevil to start off an infestation. Control is by catching the slow-moving adults at night, squashing any grubs that you find or applying biological controls. If you prefer to sleep at night, there is also a chemical control for vine weevil grubs that is applied as a drench to the compost of container plants.

Vine weevil larvae attack the roots while the parents eat holes in the leaves. They are becoming a big pest of shrubs and climbers.

Scale insects

These sap-sucking insects are immobile once they have found a suitable plant. Looking like round, raised spots on the stem or bark, they appear and hold on like miniature limpets.

Small numbers can be prised off individually. If you have a bad infestation, you can gain some control by rubbing over the affected stems with some soft soap. You can also use a suitable systemic insecticide to control these pests.

Galls

Many shrubs and climbers can be affected by galls, which appear as raised lumps on the upper or lower leaf surface and are caused by insects. The plant itself is stimulated by the insect to produce the odd-looking growths that can be either brightly coloured or well camouflaged. The main groups of insects that cause plants to produce galls are gall-wasps, gall-midges and gall-mites. They generally lay eggs inside the gall so that the hatching grub is protected by the plant as it feeds. In one particular type of attack by gall-mites, witches brooms are produced.

Control is unnecessary. If the galls are unsightly, cut off the affected foliage. On deciduous plants, rake up and bin the leaves at the end of the season in question.

Leaf-cutter bees

Semi-circular notches in the leaves of roses, privet and laburnums can be attributed to the activities of leaf-cutter bees, which collect material to build their nests.

The females get busy in early summer building individual cells out of pieces cut from suitable foliage.

The pest is a solitary bee that doesn't swarm or sting, and so is otherwise perfectly harmless. Little damaged is caused and no control is necessary. Unsightly leaves can be picked off if required.

Leaf miners

Tunnels, blotches and other leaf blemishes are caused by the grubs of certain insects. Different insects attack different types of plants. For example, the holly leaf miner causes unsightly tunnelling and brown areas in the fleshy leaves of this plant, which are caused by the grub of a fly. This can be a particular nuisance on hedges and hollies cut for indoor arrangements.

Different species of moth caterpillar cause similar damage to laburnums, gorse, lilac and other ornamental plants during early summer. Control is rarely called for because the plants are largely unaffected. However, if you want to stop further damage to hedges and prominent plants, dispose of hedge clippings and fallen leaves carefully, clear weeds that can harbour these pests and spray with a suitable systemic insecticide.

Dealing with diseases

The most prevalent diseases affect a wide range of different plants. Their spread depends both on the vigour of the shrub or climber being attacked and also on the prevailing weather conditions.

Plant health

There are many different diseases that can affect your plants. Most of these are quite rare but every garden will suffer from its share of diseases at some point. In the main, most of these diseases are relatively easy to deal with, if you have made the correct diagnosis. As ever, it is best to be able to prevent disease rather than allowing it to take hold and spread in your garden.

The best way to control pests and diseases is to stay one step ahead of them and prevent them from becoming a problem in the first place. Stay vigilant at all times, so that when they do occur, you will be able to take decisive action quickly and effectively.

How to prevent pests and diseases

Practise good garden hygiene and you will go a long way to preventing outbreaks of pests and diseases. Clearing away fallen leaves and other debris and consigning any diseased material to the dustbin or bonfire, will help to prevent these problems carrying over from one year to the next.

It is also a good idea to keep weeds under control, which often act as a sink of infection. Always keep your eyes open for the first signs of pest and disease attack. When you are moving among your plants when watering, weeding or feeding, for instance, stay vigilant for tell-tale signs and symptoms of disease. Check them at night, too, since some serious pests, including slugs and vine weevils, are more active at night than they are at other times.

If you see anything untoward, take action quickly so that you can nip stop any problems before they spread and become more serious. Individual pests can be picked up and destroyed, while isolated outbreaks of disease can be pruned off the plant. Similarly, initial colonies of small insects such as aphids can be rubbed out between you finger and thumb. You can also stay one step ahead of the pests and diseases by putting down traps and barriers.

Powdery mildew

These are white, dusty-looking deposits that can be found on the young leaves and stems of plants, usually on the upper surface, causing their growth to become stunted and discoloured. It is caused by a range of fungi. Attacks are most acute during long, dry spells.
Treatment Remove and destroy any affected foliage and keep susceptible plants well watered during drought. Weed carefully, as the disease can be spread by weeds. Spray with a suitable systemic fungicide.

Downy mildew

Usually seen as yellow patches on the leaves, with grey or purple mould growing on the undersides, downy mildew is most prevalent in mild and damp weather.
Treatment Pick off and destroy any of the affected stems and try to encourage more air flow to flow between the plants by spacing them more widely. Spray healthy looking leaves with a suitable systemic fungicide to prevent a recurrence.

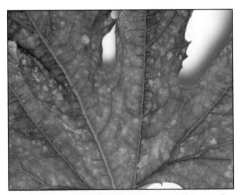

Powdery mildew looks like a dusty white-grey coating. It causes stunting and distortion of leaves, buds, growing tips and fruit.

Rust is a common fungal disease. Rusty patches or spots appear on the leaves, distorting growth and causing leaf drop.

Blackspot is a fungal disease that particularly affects roses. Black spots appear, primarily on the leaves, but sometimes on the stems.

The distinctive pinkish pustules of coral spot. The fungus enters through small wounds in the plant, usually caused by careless pruning.

Nutrient deficiencies

When plants run short of one or more particular nutrients, it can show up as leaf symptoms that are easy to confuse with disease symptoms. Magnesium and manganese deficiencies, for example, both cause yellowing between the leaf veins, while potash deficiency often causes the leaf edges to yellow or leaf tips to scorch.

The other two main plant nutrients, nitrogen and phosphorus, are more difficult to spot, causing poor, often pale, growth with small leaves that are sometimes discoloured. Fortunately, all these problems are easy to put right by feeding: use a balanced general fertilizer for the three main nutrients and one containing trace elements to supply your plants with extra magnesium and manganese.

Blackspot

This disease causes dark spots on the leaves, often with a yellow edge, which can lead to premature leaf drop. It is a serious disease when it affects roses, as it can severely weaken the plant if it is allowed to flourish year after year.

Treatment To control it, remove and destroy any affected foliage and clear fallen leaves in autumn to help prevent the continuation of the disease. This may mean hard-pruning infected plants. Spray healthy-looking leaves with a suitable systemic fungicide.

Rust

This is a common fungal disease that causes distinctive bright orange to brown spots on the undersides of leaves, with yellow flecks on the upper surface. The spots will eventually darken to black and the symptoms can sometimes spread to nearby plant stems.

Different species of rust attack different plants, with roses being particularly affected.

Treatment To control rust, remove and destroy any affected foliage and clear fallen leaves in autumn to help prevent the disease continuing. Try to avoid overhead watering, as the rust spores can be carried back up to the plant by the splashing water. Instead, apply the water at the base of the plant. Spray healthy-looking leaves with a suitable systemic fungicide as necessary.

Leaf spots

There are several types of leaf spot, some with dark green, brown or black spots, sometimes round, sometimes angular, on leaf surfaces. Coral spot, for example, has distinctive small, coral-coloured pustules. A host of fungi can be responsible, but the problem will only be temporary.

Treatment Prune out affected growth if you find it unsightly and feed the plant to encourage vigorous new shoots. Generally, it is not usually worth spraying for these spots, but if you want you can tackle them by using a suitable systemic fungicide.

Downy mildew appears as a white coating over leaves and causes distended growth, browning and wilting.

Grey mould

Also known as botrytis, this disease causes fluffy grey mould to appear on buds, flowers, leaves or stems and can occur on nearly any garden plant. However, it can be problematic with large flowers that 'ball' in wet weather and rot, as well as leaves and stems that have been damaged before the attack.

Treatment Pick off affected flowers and shoots and clear fallen ripe fruit, which can also be attacked. Make sure the plants are well spaced and ventilated to prevent a recurrence.

Powdery mildew appears as a dusty-looking coating on the plant. Dry soil and warm, humid, stagnant air encourage it.

Keep plants well watered. Cut off any affected shoots and improve air circulation around the plant. Spray with a systemic fungicide.

Methods of control

All pests are preyed upon by natural predators in the garden, including birds, small mammals, amphibians, spiders and insects. One of the best ways of keeping pests under control is to encourage these natural predators to set up home.

Not all insects are pests in the garden. The ladybird is one of many that feed on garden problem pests and help keep their damaging populations under control.

Encourage natural predators

Welcome nature's way of controlling pests to your garden. For example, you can get frogs and toads, which feed on a wide range of insects, to remain by providing them with suitable places to hide and a small pond where they can breed. Similarly, many beneficial insects, such as hoverflies and lacewings, will be attracted by nectar-rich plants, such as buddleja, hawthorn and viburnum, and can be encouraged to overwinter by putting up bundles of bamboo where they can hibernate.

Other creatures to encourage include ladybirds (ladybugs), which eat aphids, scale insects, mealy bugs and caterpillars; ground beetles, which consume slugs, troublesome flatworms, vine weevils and spider mites; and centipedes, which eat slugs and snails.

The following are good predators to invite into your garden.

Ladybirds (Ladybugs) A single ladybird larva is able to eat more than 500 aphids while it is developing, so for this reason alone, ladybirds can have a dramatic impact on these pest numbers. Ladybird larvae look nothing like the familiar black-spotted red adult but look like a cross between a beetle and a caterpillar – so make sure you know what they look like so that you don't inadvertently think it's another pest to control.

Lacewings These are green flying insects that have translucent green wings, long antennae and bright, golden eyes. Both the adults and larvae feed on aphids. The larvae are similar to ladybird larvae, but they are lighter in colour and often have dead aphids stuck to their bodies to act as camouflage.

Hover flies These are insects that mimic the appearance of wasps but are smaller and able to hover in one spot. They don't sting. As their name implies, they are true flies and their larvae eat aphids and other small sap-sucking insects.

Ground beetles Some beetles are troublesome in the garden, but the big black beetles that scurry about at night are ground beetles and they are definitely worth encouraging as they are voracious eaters of slugs and other insects.

Centipedes Often confused with millipedes, which can damage plants, centipedes eat insects and are worth encouraging into the garden. One simple way to tell them apart is to touch them: a centipede will scuttle away as fast as possible, while a millipede will tend to roll itself up for protection.

Amphibians Frogs, toads and newts are all useful predators in the garden, as they gobble up slugs and insects. You will need a pond to encourage them into your garden, with suitable access and cover to provide a safe haven and breeding ground.

Hedgehogs Under the cover of darkness, hedgehogs are busy clearing gardens of slugs, caterpillars, beetles and other problem pests. Provide food and winter shelter to encourage them to set up home in your garden.

Birds Many garden birds eat pests. Starlings will eat worms and grubs; sparrows eat insects and weed seeds; thrushes love slugs and snails; robins favour spiders and weed seeds; and blue tits like caterpillars and aphids. Encourage them to stay in your garden by providing a plentiful supply of seed- and berry-producing plants, sheltered areas where they can build nests safely and rear their young, and a source of food and water during the winter months for resident species.

Using pesticides

If you choose to use pesticides to control pest and disease outbreaks, you must read the instructions carefully to ensure that the pest you are trying to control is featured on the label. Garden chemicals are broadly divided into three groups: fungicides, which control disease; pesticides, which control pests; and herbicides, which control weeds.

Some chemicals, called contact pesticides, work only when they are applied to the target. For this reason, if you are using contact insecticides it is essential that they are applied, sprayed or dusted where the pests are lurking – often in the shoot tips and on the undersides of the leaves. Some contact pesticides will remain active for a period of time to control pests and diseases that try to attack the plant for up to a fortnight after being applied. Others, known as systemic chemicals, are absorbed by the plant and transported throughout its structure via the sap. Such chemicals can be applied anywhere on the plant to control the pests and diseases attacking it. This means you can spray less accurately and do not need to cover all the foliage completely. A few chemical fungicidal sprays can be applied to

Using chemicals as a last resort

If all else fails and your plants are plagued by a damaging attack, you may want to resort to using a chemical spray. It is essential that you choose the right spray for the job and apply it exactly as described in the information on the packaging. However, you may also want to keep a few chemicals to hand, locked away safely in the garden shed or garage, that can be used in an emergency. It's worth having a packet of slug pellets if you want to protect vulnerable new plants, and a general systemic insecticide is handy for combating insect pests.

plants before the disease has attacked to provide protection. These are known as preventative fungicides. Like contact chemicals, they have to be applied thoroughly to give complete protection. Check the label carefully for instructions about how often the product should be reapplied and follow this diligently if you want it to be effective. Roses are a good example of how using a combined pesticide and fungicide produces healthy blooms.

Applying chemicals

Garden pesticides are available in various forms. Ready-to-use sprays that are already diluted are the most convenient form and, as their name suggests, can be applied immediately. They are an expensive way to buy pesticides, but they are useful if you are trying to control a small outbreak quickly, such as a pest outbreak in the greenhouse.

In the longer term, it might be preferable to invest in a small hand-pumped pressure sprayer in which to dilute concentrated chemicals. These work out much cheaper if you are applying a lot of the same chemical over the course of a season. Sprayers with a lance will also apply the chemical more quickly and accurately to border plants. For really large gardens, consider investing in a knapsack sprayer, which is much larger and enables you to spray for longer between refills.

Weedkillers are applied differently, depending on where the seeds are located. On a gravel path, for example, you could water the weedkiller using a watering can fitted with a dribble bar, but in the border you would be better off using a sprayer fitted with a spray hood to prevent any spray drift affecting neighbouring plants. Simply place

Healthy roses

The best way to keep roses healthy is to grow disease-resistant roses (see below). However, you can prevent the three common rose diseases of blackspot, mildew and rust on less robust varieties by following a regular spraying programme. If you use a combined pesticide and fungicide that is designed for the purpose, you can prevent outbreaks of pests such as aphids, too. Roses also benefit from a foliar feed containing trace elements to keep the foliage green and healthy.

The following varieties have all shown some resistance to blackspot, mildew and rust:
Large-flowered bush roses
'Alec's Red', 'Alexander', 'Blessings', 'Congratulations', 'Just Joey', 'Peace', 'Polar Star' (not rust), 'Remember Me', 'Royal William' and 'Silver Jubilee'.
Cluster-flowered bush rose
'Amber Queen', 'Mountbatten', 'Queen Elizabeth' (not blackspot) and 'Southampton'.
Climbing roses
'Aloha', 'Compassion', 'Golden Showers' and 'New Dawn'.

the hood over the weed, with the rim on the ground, before pressing the trigger to release the chemical spray. Set the spray nozzle to produce a coarse spray to minimize any airborne droplets.

Safety first

Always read the label carefully before you buy or use a garden pesticide to make sure it will do what you want. Take great care to apply it at the right dilution and observe any precautions that are recommended. Always wear the protective clothing suggested when handling chemicals. Dispose of unwanted garden chemicals at your local authority's waste disposal centre.

Calendar of care

Most of the essential tasks in ornamental gardens are seasonal and so have to be carried out at a certain time of the year. With many shrubs and climbers the most important job is pruning, which has to be carried out at the right stage of growth to prevent flowering production or loss in the following season. On the following pages you will find a comprehensive guide to what to prune and when.

There is also a quick-reference checklist to all the other seasonal tasks, including propagating, planting, feeding, watering, weeding and protecting, so that you can be sure to complete all necessary tasks at the right time of the year. If you are short of time, prioritize your gardening workload to make sure that the most critical tasks are carried out first.

It should be remembered that the beginning and end of the seasons varies from year to year as well as with your local climate, so the exact timing should depend on how your plants are growing at the time. For example, a spring-flowering plant in a sheltered garden in a relatively warm country can flower up to four weeks earlier than the same plant growing in a more exposed spot elsewhere.

Note: In the pruning calendars for shrubs and climbers featured on the following pages, plants featured in more than one month can be pruned at any time in this period.

The gardener's tasks continue throughout the year, making sure that each season yields the best show of flowers and foliage, providing a rich reward for all the work that it entails.

Seasonal jobs checklist: spring and summer

Spring is when the garden starts to come alive again, and there are a number of tasks awaiting your attention, which are listed here.

Things to do in spring
- Check plants for winter damage
- Firm in any new plants loosened by winter frosts
- Water all new additions
- Trim winter-flowering heathers
- Plant new shrubs and climbers
- Plant evergreen and deciduous hedging
- Keep control of weeds
- Complete rose pruning
- Complete renovation of overgrown shrubs and climbers
- Check supports of all climbers
- Apply a general fertilizer to established plants
- Propagate by layering
- Sow seeds collected last summer and given cold treatment over winter
- Take leaf-bud cuttings
- Take softwood cuttings
- Separate rooted layers from parent plants and pot up or plant out
- Watch out for pests and disease
- Tie in new stems of climbers as they grow
- Prune early flowering shrubs
- Prune grey-leaved shrubs
- Prune evergreens
- Trim formal edging shrubs
- Start clipping hedges

What to prune in spring

Early spring shrubs
Artemisia
Buddleja davidii
Colutea
Convolvulus cneorum
Cotinus
Daphne (after flowering)
Forsythia (after flowering)
Fothergilla (after flowering)
Griselinia
Hamamellis (after flowering)
Hebe cupressoides
Hebe pinguifolia
Hebe rakaiensis
Hydrangea arborescens
Hydrangea paniculata
Hypericum calycinum
Lavatera
Mahonia (after flowering)
Rhus
Ribes sanguineum (after flowering)
Rosa
Skimmia (after flowering)
Spiraea japonica
Symphoricarpos
Viburnum farreri (after flowering)
Viburnum opulus (after flowering)
Vinca

Early spring climbers
Cissus
Clematis (Group 3)
Cobaea
Eccremocarpus
Hedera
Humulus
Jasminum nudiflorum (after flowering)
Lonicera

Mid-spring shrubs
Abutilon megapotanum
Aucuba (fruiting)
Callicarpa
Calluna
Camellia (after flowering)
Caryopteris
Ceanothus 'Autumnal Blue'
Ceanothus 'Burkwoodii'
Ceratostigma
Cistus
Clerodendrum bungei
Corylopsis (after flowering)
Cotoneaster frigidus 'Cornubia'
Cotoneaster x watereri
Erica (after flowering)
Euonymus japonicus
Euphorbia pulcherrima (after flowering)
Exochorda (after flowering)
Fatsia
Forsythia (after flowering)
Hebe macrantha,
Hebe salicifolia
Hebe speciosa
Helichrysum
Hydrangea macrophylla
Hydrangea serrata
Hypericum 'Hidcote'
Kerria (after flowering)
Lavandula
Leycesteria
Ligustrum
Lonicera fragrantissima (after flowering)
Lonicera x purpusii (after flowering)
Olearia
Osmanthus (after flowering)
Perovskia
Phygelius

Pieris (after flowering)
Pittosporum
Potentilla
Pyracantha

Mid-spring climbers
Cissus
Passiflora
Solanum

Late spring shrubs
Abelia
Akebia quinata
Chaenomeles (after flowering)
Choisya (after flowering)
Helichrysum petiolare
Hibiscus
Ribes speciosum (after flowering)

Late-spring climbers
Berberidopsis
Cissus
Clematis (group 1, after flowering)

Prune cistus plants, including the *Cistus* x *skanbergii* shown here, after flowering.

What to prune in summer

Early summer shrubs
Berberis darwinii (after flowering)
Berberis linearifolia (after flowering)
Berberis x *stenophylla* (after flowering)
Cornus kousa var. *chinensis*
Cornus mas
Cornus officinalis
Cytisus x *praecox* (after flowering)
Deutzia (after flowering)
Helichrysum petiolare
Hippophae
Magnolia liliiflora
Magnolia x *soulangeana*
Magnolia stellata
Rosmarinus (after flowering)
Spiraea 'Arguta' (after flowering)
Syringa (after flowering)

Mid-summer climbers
Clematis (group 1, after flowering)

Mid-summer shrubs
Buxus
Carpenteria
Ceanothus arboreus 'Trewithen Blue'
  (after flowering)
Ceanothus 'Concha' (after flowering)
Ceanothus impressus (after flowering)
Ceanothus thyrsiflorus (after flowering)
Cytisus battandieri (after flowering)
Escallonia 'Apple Blossom' (after
  flowering)

Euphorbia characias (after flowering)
Euphorbia myrsinites (after flowering)
Fremontodendron (after flowering)
Helianthemum (after flowering)
Helichrysum petiolare
Kolkwitzia (after flowering)
Laurus
Lonicera nitida
Paeonia (after flowering)
Philadelphus microphyllus (after flowering)
Rhododendron luteum (after flowering)
Rubus cockburnianus (after flowering)
Sophora
Tamarix (after flowering)
Tinus (after flowering)
Viburnum plicatum (after flowering)
Weigela (after flowering)

Mid-summer climbers
Wisteria

Late summer shrubs
Buddleja alternifolia (after flowering)
Buxus
Callistemon (after flowering)
Elaeagnus x *ebbinge*
Elaeagnus glabra
Elaeagnus macrophylla
Elaeagnus pungens 'Maculata'
x *Fatshedera*
Genista hispanica (after flowering)
Grevillea (after flowering)

Helianthemum (after flowering)
Laurus
Nerium
Philadelphus 'Belle Etoile' (after
  flowering)
Philadelphus coronarius (after flowering)
Philadelphus delavayi (after flowering)
Philadelphus 'Virginal' (after flowering)
Pyracantha
Thymus

Late summer climbers
Billardiera (after fruiting)
Clerodendrum (after flowering)
Clianthus (after flowering)
Hydrangea (after flowering)
Jasminum polyanthum (after flowering)

Prune Clematis Group 1 plants in late spring, like the *Clematis armandii* shown here.

Summer is when you can really enjoy the fruits of your labours and revel in the splendour of your garden. It is also a time of plant maintenance, so that you can keep your garden looking its very best and allowing your shrubs and climbers to dazzle.

Trim hedges like *Osmanthus heterophyllus* 'Tricolor'. Cut out any reverted leaves on variegated types when you see them.

Things to do in summer
- Water all new additions
- Take semi-ripe cuttings
- Move out tender plants to a sheltered position outdoors
- Prune early clematis
- Prune climbers and wall shrubs after flowering
- Prune early summer-flowering shrubs after flowering
- Clear ground for autumn planting
- Spray against rose diseases
- Pot up rooted cuttings taken in the spring
- Deadhead large-flowered shrubs after flowering
- Remove suckers from roses
- Trim conifer hedges
- Train climbing and rambler roses
- Trim lavender after flowering
- Harvest lavender for drying
- Maintain control over pest and disease outbreaks
- Summer prune wisteria
- Keep weeds under control
- Cut out any reverted shoots on variegated shrubs and climbers
- Prune rambler roses after flowering

Seasonal jobs checklist: autumn and winter

Early autumn, if it is kind, can provide an Indian summer in the garden, prolonging the flowering times of your shrubs and climbers. Gradually, glorious leaf shades appear on the plants, providing a spectacular last display before dropping in mid- to late autumn.

What to do in autumn

- Take hardwood cuttings
- Pot on semi-ripe cuttings taken in summer
- Prune late-flowering shrubs
- Part-prune tall shrubs to prevent wind rock
- Plant new shrubs, climbers and hedges
- Trim vigorous hedges
- Keep weeds under control
- Tie in whippy shoots on climbers
- Collect seed and berries for propagation
- Protect borderline hardy shrubs and climbers
- Bring tender plants under cover before the first frosts
- Propagate from suitable stems by layering
- Clear away diseased leaves from roses

Autumn is the time for pruning in the garden. Vigorously growing hedges can take quite a bold cutting back at this time of year.

- Take root cuttings
- Plant deciduous shrubs and climbers
- Protect container-grown hardy shrubs and climbers, if necessary
- Take root cuttings
- Dig over vacant ground when soil conditions allow
- Move awkwardly placed shrubs and climbers or those that you wish to relocate elsewhere in the garden
- Check tree ties and stakes and replace if necessary
- Take measures to make sure nothing can be damaged on windy nights
- Plant shrubs, roses and hedging plants that are sold with bare roots

What to prune in autumn

EARLY AUTUMN
Shrubs
Abelia (after flowering)
Buxus
Lonicera nitida
Nerium

Climbers
Jasminum officinale (after flowering)
Lathyrus latifolius (after flowering)
Lonicera periclymenum
Lonicera x *americana*
Lonicera x *brownii*
Lonicera x *tellmanniana*
Passiflora (after flowering)
Rosa (climbing, after flowering)

MID-AUTUMN
Shrubs
Santolina (after flowering)

Climbers
Parthenocissus

LATE AUTUMN
Shrubs
Amelanchier
Aucuba (non-fruiting)

Climbers
Parthenocissus

Autumn produces spectacular colour displays, as shown by *Calluna vulgaris* 'Wickwar Flame'.

Winter is usually a dormant time in the garden, although there is still much to do. The main aim in winter is to protect plants from the ravages of wind, frost and snowfalls. However, it is also a time for the pruning and propagation of certain shrubs and climbers.

What to do in winter

- Clear heavy falls of snow off hedges and evergreens, if necessary
- Take hardwood cuttings from roses
- Prune climbing roses
- If it's a mild winter, continue to cut the lawn, as long as it is still growing, but raise the height of the mower blades
- Prevent container-grown plants from freezing by wrapping them with bubble wrap or taking them under shelter
- Remove algae and moss patches on the patio and paving by scrubbing with a broom or blasting with a pressure washer
- Feed indoor plants occasionally
- Order seed catalogues and look on the internet to plan what you're going to grow in the spring
- Winter prune wisteria
- Carry out all winter pruning jobs
- Protect berried holly branches to preserve fruit for winter decoration
- Protect new additions with windbreak netting
- Renovate overgrown shrubs and climbers
- Prune tall-growing bush roses by about a half to help prevent wind-rock damaging roots, and shorten all the branches on standard roses for the same reason
- Plant bare-rooted rose bushes
- Water plants sparingly
- Be on the watch for any pests on overwintering plants and destroy them

What to prune in winter

EARLY WINTER
Shrubs
Amelanchier
Aucuba (non-fruiting)
Berberis thunbergii
Berberis x ottawensis
Salix caprea 'Kilmarnock'
Sambucus

Climbers
Ampelopsis
Parthenocissus
Vitis
Wisteria

MID-WINTER
Shrubs
Aucuba (non-fruiting)
Cotoneaster horizontalis
Salix caprea 'Kilmarnock'
Sambucus

Climbers
Actinidia
Ampelopsis
Bougainvillea
Campsis
Celastrus
Mandevilla
Vitis
Wisteria

LATE WINTER
Shrubs
Aucuba (non-fruiting)
Buddleja globosa
Chimonathus (after flowering)
Cornus alba
Cornus sanguinea
Cornus stolonifera
Corylus
Cotoneaster dammeri
Cotoneaster microphyllus
Euonymus europaeus
Euonymus alatus
Garrya ellipticus (after flowering)
Rosa (bush)
Sambucus

Climbers
Actinidia
Bougainvillea
Campsis
Clematis (Group 2 & Group 3)
Hedera
Humulus
Jasminum nudiflorum (after flowering)
Lonicera japonica
Lonicera henryi
Rubus

Keep the heat in the greenhouse by covering the glass panes with bubble wrap. This will help to insulate it and retain heat. Use a foil covering under the wrap on the shady side.

Index

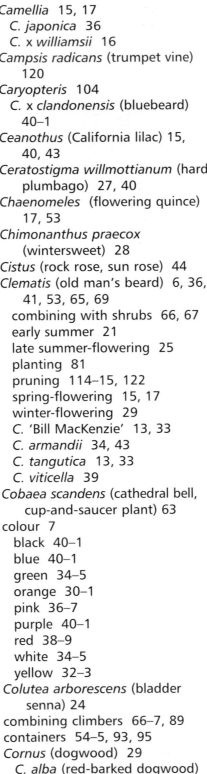

Acknowledgements
Unless listed below,
photographs are © Anness
Publishing Ltd.

The publishers would like to
thank Peter Anderson for his
work on the original
photography.
Andrew Lawson Photography:
124–5; 142–3; 152–3.